A
HISTORY OF
EVERYDAY THINGS
IN ENGLAND

1 Norman Costume. Twelfth Century

A
HISTORY OF
EVERYDAY THINGS
IN ENGLAND

Volume I
1066 to 1499

By

MARJORIE & C. H. B. QUENNELL

LONDON
B. T. BATSFORD LTD

First Published 1918
Eleventh Impression (Fourth Edition) 1957

To
P. C. Q.
G. E. Q.
&
R. P. Q.

PRINTED AND BOUND IN GREAT BRITAIN BY JARROLD AND SONS LTD
LONDON AND NORWICH
FOR THE PUBLISHERS
B. T. BATSFORD LTD
4 FITZHARDINGE STREET, PORTMAN SQUARE, LONDON, W.I

2 The Coronation of Harold

PREFACE

THE first volume of *A History of Everyday Things in England* made its original appearance during October 1918. The date is significant. For my father, already a middle-aged man, who between 1900 and 1914 had practised with increasing success as a domestic architect, the War had been both a professional reverse and a spiritual calamity. An inheritor of the constructive ideals of John Ruskin and William Morris, he had watched the forces of destruction raging all around him; his own career had been suddenly cut short; and the "war-work" he was obliged to take up proved particularly dull and uncongenial. Rather than accept defeat, he decided that he would write a book—a method of self-expression he had never attempted before, although he had contributed a good many articles to weekly and monthly papers that dealt with architectural subjects. The book was written at home, usually after he had returned from his office; and his study was the family living-room where, under a greenish sputtering gas-mantle, he and my devoted mother occupied adjacent desks. Their collaboration was close and harmonious. The basic idea had been supplied by my father, an expert technical draughtsman whose province included castles, houses, waggons, ships and windmills; but my mother provided details of costume and armour and many other aspects of everyday life; and, as soon as my father had sketched out an illustration, he relied on my mother's skill to people its foreground with animated contemporary figures.

PREFACE

Thus the first volume gradually took shape—a volume intended not only to re-create the past, which he had always loved and reverenced, but to express his faith in the present day and his hopes for future generations. The War was ending; and tremendous opportunities, he wrote on his original Introduction, would await the young men of the post-war age. But, if they were to become "constructors and craftsmen, able and deserving to carry on the work of the world, they must obtain a good store of knowledge—lay hold of tradition, so that they can benefit by what has been done—know that in one direction progress can be made, and that in another it will be arrested". They must learn to combine the wonderful appreciation of the "uses and beauty of material which the old craftsmen possessed, with the opportunities for production which the modern machine gives", and so prepare the way for a "new era of beautiful everyday things".

When the book had at length been written and illustrated, it was entrusted to my father's old friend, that versatile and gifted publisher, the late Harry Batsford. Neither the author nor the publisher, I think, then expected to reap a very large reward. They were wrong. *Everyday Things* began to sell rapidly, and has been selling ever since. Few books of the period can claim to have been in continuous demand for the last thirty-eight years; and its sale was not diminished by the outbreak of the Second World War, which, happily for himself perhaps, my father did not live to see. Such is the influence of a simple but sound idea, applied in bold and straightforward fashion by an enthusiastic and disinterested writer! To-day, having run through ten impressions and three editions, *Everyday Things* has again been reprinted; and I have been asked to look through the text and make some minor corrections and editorial re-arrangements. These changes have not been extensive; and throughout I have done my best to preserve the original spirit and form. From some points of view, the book is a self-portrait —the portrait of a modest and generous man who believed passionately in Ruskin's Gospel of Work and in the honesty, decency and intrinsic goodwill of his fellow human beings.

PETER QUENNELL

October 1956.

CONTENTS

ACKNOWLEDGMENT

THE authors and publishers wish to thank the authorities of the British Museum, the Victoria and Albert Museum at South Kensington and the Bodleian Library, Oxford, for the reproduction of various subjects, including illuminated MSS. Fig. 88 is included by permission of the Fitzwilliam Museum, Cambridge, and Figs. 30–3 are reproduced, by permission, from MSS. in Trinity College, Cambridge. Some of the material relating to Beaumaris Castle, together with the isometric view and three drawings of siege engines, is, with the approval of the author, inserted from *The English Castle*, by Mr. Hugh Braun, F.S.A. Figs. 13 and 107 are from drawings by Mr. Sydney R. Jones in works issued by the publishers, and thanks are due to Mrs. W. H. Paterson for Figs. 141–2 from the book on *Medieval Gardens* by her father, Sir F. Crisp.

INTRODUCTION

THIS is a History of Everyday Things in England, from the time of the Norman Conquest in 1066 down to the end of the eighteenth century. It is an account of the work of the people, rather than of the politics that guided them.

Now as to why this book has been written. In the first place, anything that helps to give us a picture of bygone times must make the history of the period more interesting, and we cannot have a picture without a background. It is only fair to the characters of history that we set our stage for them as well as we can; provide them with the proper costumes and setting; give them adequate background, against which they can strut and play their part, and make their bow to us before they go.

By adequate background we do not mean just a *pictorial* setting. We must also seek to discover how they passed their time; the kind of work they did; the things they used.

A study of Everyday Things will help us to understand the life of a period. In our own country are still preserved the everyday things of many different centuries—sometimes ruined, sometimes so much altered that it is a little difficult to understand what they were like originally. But by taking a fragment here, and another there, it is possible to piece together the whole; and this is what we have had to do.

So far as we have been able, we have drawn the same everyday things in each century: Costume, Ships, Castles, Houses, Halls, Monasteries, Carts, Games, Ornaments, so that a series of parallels can be drawn between the centuries; and at the beginning of each chapter a chart is given which links up the work done with the people who did it.

It has always seemed extraordinary to the writers that boys and girls in England grow up without having learned very much about the surroundings of history. School books are, of course, illustrated; and here and there an enthusiastic master will take up architecture perhaps as a side-line; but, generally speaking, boys and girls leave school without even knowing the names of the styles. Think of the excitement there would be if the end of Jocelin of Brakelond's Chronicle were ever found; yet we neglect the remains of Benedictine monasteries all over the country, as having no real educational value. We avail ourselves of Matthew Paris's history; but we are not interested in his home at St. Albans.

Then there is the constructional side of all the crafts. Work developed in a wonderful way when it was a living art, done joyfully by men and women with their hands and a few simple tools.

In the medieval period the arts and crafts were much more representative of the whole community than they are now. The craftsman learnt not only the practical details of his trade, the way to use his tools, and to select materials, but was taught to design his work; and all his fellows did the same, working together on much the same lines—all interested in doing good work, and in trying to find better methods and designs. This accumulated knowledge was handed down from generation to generation, and formed what we call tradition; and, thanks to it, the work produced was extraordinarily truthful. The man of the fourteenth century was not content to copy the work done in the thirteenth, but, with all his fellows, was trying to improve on it. So, if we have sufficient knowledge, we can recognise the details, and say this place must have been built at such a date.

Gothic architecture was like a strong tree, deeply rooted in the past, always growing; and when the Renaissance came in the sixteenth century, much the same thing happened—craftsmen gradually accepted the new tradition and carried it on; and so it continued until the end of the eighteenth century. Then the introduction of machinery had a very disturbing effect; for quite suddenly men found that it was possible to produce in bulk. The machine is only adapted to repetition; and, instead of many men working and designing together, a single man became the designer, all the others being put to looking after the machines, with the result that the standard of design has degenerated. There must be something in this; or you would not find that collectors will give almost any money for old furniture and silver, and hardly anything at all for second-hand machine-made imitations. This is a terrible state of affairs. We have so few people designing and creating, and so many machine-tenders, that as we cannot produce a sufficient stream of energy to develop a tradition of our own; and we fall back

12

on copying, and talk about "Elizabethan" houses, and, worse than all, we build sham Gothic churches. To-day, after the destruction wrought by two world wars, we hope that we are entering a period of construction. There is a new spirit abroad; we all want to make the world a better place to live in, with wider opportunities and greater consideration for good citizens. Cottages are wanted for the countryside. Our towns have to be made clean and tidy, without raw ends as now, dedicated to tin cans and rubbish heaps; good healthy houses, which can be made into homes, must take the place of the slums, and fine schools and public buildings must show that we have gained in civic spirit. People demand a well-ordered existence in which they can do useful and interesting work, not necessarily for just themselves, but including some service for others.

Boys and girls who are now growing up will be given opportunities that no other generation has ever had; and it is of the greatest importance that they should be trained to do useful work and learn to use their hands. Before they can become actual constructors and craftsmen, able and worthy to carry on the work of the world, they must obtain a good store of knowledge—lay hold of tradition, so that they can benefit by what has been done—know that in one direction progress can be made, and that in another it will be arrested. Thus the coming generation may combine the wonderful appreciation for the uses and beauty of material that the old craftsmen possessed, with the opportunities for production which the modern machine gives, and so launch a new era of beautiful everyday things.

If our book helps a little in this direction then we shall be well repaid for our trouble. It must be taken, however, as an outline sketch only; but it is hoped that it will be found sufficiently entertaining to stimulate the interest of its readers, and set them to work in the same direction. Our coloured costume-plates, for example, have been drawn to show figures characteristic of the beginning, middle and end of each century; and, once our readers have the broad outline of the development of dress fixed in their minds, by examining monuments, pictures, and brasses in churches they can fill in the gaps themselves, and will enjoy noticing local variations and fashions. Armour is another delightful subject that has been no more than touched on; and heraldry had to be left out altogether. We should have liked to say far more about the Normans, their marvellous activities, their work and travels. Here, again, is an interesting subject for independent research.

Much more might have been said in detail about pottery, jewellery, ships, and all the hundred and one things that were used in olden times; but, so far as is possible, we have endeavoured to show these as part of a whole in the pictures. This, again, is a point that our readers can settle for themselves; they can tackle the detail of the subject first, and work up to its wider interest after; or, taking our book as a general sketch, select details which attract them for independent study. The great thing is the broad range of life in bygone times.

So many people have made kindly suggestions that it is a little difficult to acknowledge suitably our obligations; but we should like to express our indebtedness to Mr. H. W. Burrows, for the loan of careful measured drawings of an old Essex mill, from which the illustration of the Fifteenth-century Windmill was made; to Mr. Cecil C. Brewer, for the loan of drawings of Castle Hedingham; and to Mr. H. F. T. Cooper, for the use of a very interesting chart showing the relation of the Arts to History, from which we have gained much useful information. We are as well greatly indebted to Miss Irene J. Churchill, for the loan of many books and for her kindly help. We desire to make special mention of the assistance we have received from Mr. R. Morton Nance in the preparation of our Ship Drawings, which, as a result of his great knowledge and kindly criticism, look a little more like the real thing than they did originally

M. & C. H. B. Q.

BIBLIOGRAPHY

W E give below a list of books that our readers are recommended to consult if they want fuller information on any particular subject.

F. M. Kelly and R. Schwabe, *A History of English Costume and Armour.*
D. Yarwood, *English Costume; 200 B.C. to 1952.*
James Laver, *Costume* (Junior Heritage Series).
D. Gorsline, *What People Wore.*

Castles

Charles H. Ashdown, *British Castles.*
Hugh Braun, *The English Castle.*
R. Allen Brown, *English Medieval Castles.*
R. Allen Brown, *Castles* (Junior Heritage Series).

Churches

Francis Bond, *Gothic Architecture in England.*
H. Felton and J. Harvey, *The English Cathedrals.*
Cox and Ford, *The Parish Churches of England.*
Batsford and Fry, *The Greater English Church.*
F. H. Crossley, *English Church Craftsmanship.*
F. H. Crossley, *English Church Design.*
A. H. Gardner, *Outline of English Architecture.*
A. J. Stratton, *Styles of English Architecture.*
J. H. Harvey, *Henry Yevele: An English Mediæval Architect.*
A. Needham, *How to Study an Old Church.*
Edmund Vale, *Churches* (Junior Heritage Series).
Edmund Vale, *Cathedrals* (Junior Heritage Series).

Furniture

Macquoid, *History of English Furniture.*
H. Cescinsky, *Early English Furniture and Woodwork.*
D. Smith, *Old Furniture and Woodwork.*

Houses

T. Hudson Turner, *Domestic Architecture in England.*
R. Dutton, *The English Country House.*
Thomas Wright, *Homes of Other Days.*
Gotch, *Growth of the English House.*
"Country Life."
N. Lloyd, *History of the English House.*
Batsford and Fry, *The English Cottage.*
G. Jekyll and S. R. Jones, *Old English Household Life.*
Edward Osmond, *Houses* (Junior Heritage Series).
Reginald Turner, *The Smaller English House.*

Libraries

J. W. Clark, *The Care of Books.*

15

BIBLIOGRAPHY

Monasteries

Cardinal Gasquet, *English Monastic Life.*
F. H. Crossley, *The English Abbey.*
Edmund Vale, *Abbeys and Priories* (Junior Heritage Series).

Social Life

J. Harvey, *Gothic England.*
J. Harvey, *The Plantagenets.*
H. S. Bennett, *Life on the English Manor.*
Professor G. M. Trevelyan, *English Social History.*
Dr. G. C. Coulton, *Mediæval Panorama.*
A. Abram, *Social England in the Fifteenth Century.*
The Rev. Edward L. Cutts, *Scenes and Characters of the Middle Ages.*

Ships

Holmes, *Ancient and Modern Ships*, Part I. (Ministry of Education).
E. Keble Chatterton, *Sailing Ships and their Story.*
Frank G. G. Carr, *Sea Transport* (Junior Heritage Series).

LIST OF ILLUSTRATIONS

The numerals in parentheses in the text refer to the *figure numbers*
of the illustrations

LIST OF ILLUSTRATIONS

LIST OF ILLUSTRATIONS

Dates.	Kings and Queens of England and France.	Famous Men.	Great Events, Sea Fights, and Land Battles.	Principal Buildings (B., Benedictine; C., Cistercian).
1066	William the Conqueror, *m.* Matilda of Flanders *Philip I.*, 1060	Lanfranc, Archbishop, 1070 Hereward the Wake	Battle of Hastings, 1066 Rebellion at Exeter, 1068 Waste of the North, 1069-70 Rebellion at Ely, 1071 Domesday Book, 1085	Tower of London Battle Abbey, B., 1067 St. Albans Transepts and Nave, B., 1077-93 Colchester Castle, Essex Winchester Transepts, B., 1079-93
1080		Henry of Huntingdon, historian, *b.* 1080		Ely Cathedral begun, B., 1083
1087	William Rufus	Anselm, Archbishop, 1093 Peter the Hermit	First Crusade, 1096, founded Christian kingdom at Jerusalem in 1099, which lasted eighty-eight years	Tewkesbury Abbey, B., 1087-1123 Durham Nave, B., 1093-1128 Norwich Nave, B., 1096-1119 Canterbury Choir, B., 1096
1100	Henry I., *m.* Matilda of Scotland			Westminster Hall, 1099
1106	. . . .	. . . .	Battle of Tenchebrai and Conquest of Normandy	
1108	*Louis VI.*			
1116	. . . .		War with France, 1116-19	
1117				Peterboro Nave, B., 1117-94
1119	. . . .		Battle of Brenneville	
1120			Loss of White Ship	
1125		William of Malmesbury, historian, 1095-1143		
1130	. . . .	. . . .	Norman kingdom, Sicily	Rochester Castle and Castle Hedingham, Essex
1134	. . . .		Rebellion in Wales	
1135	Stephen, *m.* Maude of Boulogne			Fountains Abbey Nave, C., 1135-45
1137	*Louis VII.*			
1138	. . . .	. . . .	Battle of the Standard	
1141			Battle of Lincoln	
1145				Rievaulx Abbey, Yorks, C.
1147			Second Crusade (St. Bernard)	Roche Abbey, Yorks, C.
1148	. . . .	. . . .	. . . .	Furness, Lancs, C.
1150				
1153	. . . .	. . . .	Treaty of Wallingford and end of Civil War	Kirkstall Abbey, Yorks, C., 1152
1154	(Plantagenet). Henry II., *m.* Eleanor of Aquitaine			Ripon Minster, Yorks, 1154-81
1158	. . . .		. . . .	Dover Castle
1159			Levy of Scutage	
1162	. . . .	Becket, made Archbishop		
1169	. . . .	. . . .	Strongbow goes to Ireland	
1170			Murder of Becket	Jervaulx Abbey, Yorks, C.
1174			Great Rebellion	Wells Cathedral begun, 1174
1177		. . . .	. . . .	Byland Abbey, Yorks, C.
1180	*Philip Augustus*			
1182		Jocelin of Brakelond's Chronicle, 1182-1202		Oakham Castle, Rutland
1187		. . . .	Saladin takes Jerusalem	
1189	Richard I., *m.* Berengaria of Navarre			
1190	. . . .	. . .	Third Crusade	
1191		Robin Hood		
1192	. . . .	. . . .	Richard in captivity	Lincoln Choir and Transepts, 1192
1194			War with France	Château Gaillard
1199	John, *m.* Isabella of Angoulême			

3   Chart of the "Norman" Period of Design, from 1066 to 1199

4   A Mounted Norman Knight

Chapter I

TWELFTH CENTURY

O UR century opens thirty-four years after the landing of
William the Conqueror and the Battle of Hastings. The
Norman Conquest was, of course, an event of tremendous
significance for England and her people. It had brought in not
only a new set of rulers but another organisation of society and
another language for the governing class.

Saxons were primarily a folk of the country, and they had
never cared to live in big towns. We see now that they had a
well-defined, if primitive, system of building churches, and we can
admire their fine illuminated manuscripts and other aspects of
their art; but they were not knit together by the firm organisation
of the feudal system, which gave the Normans a trained fighting
army that the pastoral Saxons were unable to withstand.

That magnificent piece of needlework called the "Bayeux
Tapestry", now preserved at Bayeux in Normandy, is an admirable
picture of the time and shows us the kind of ships William came
over in, the type of castles he built, the clothes and armour his
soldiers wore(1). A large copy of this wonderfully decorative

work hangs in the Victoria and Albert Museum at South Kensington.

William the Conqueror was himself an able statesman and an excellent soldier; and, although he could be extremely ruthless, as when he laid waste the northern provinces, he sought to organise and settle the country which he had invaded and conquered.

The Domesday Book is a remarkable record of the country and its resources in 1085. Throughout our century there was a great wave of church-building which covered the country with buildings great and small in a well-marked and beautiful style of Romanesque; and many hundreds of these buildings remain for us to study. There was also a very great activity in castle-building, and some of these mighty structures, such as Rochester and Hedingham, have survived the eight centuries since their erection.

Gifted men accompanied William the Conqueror or joined him later at his request, among others Lanfranc, who became Archbishop of Canterbury; and the country was organised ecclesiastically and many monasteries were built.

The firmer hold of the feudal system meant that every over-lord and every landowner was responsible for producing, when required, his appropriate number of fighting men for the king's service. One effect of the feudal system on the country folk was that many of those who farmed the lands were classed as villeins, whose status was that of serfs. But, although they were bound to their overlord, they had certain rights. Superior to them were the freemen of the cities, who gradually increased their rights and influence, usually at the cost of protracted struggles with their overlord or bishop or abbot.

As a direct result of the Norman Conquest, our island, after a lapse of some centuries, was once again brought into close and direct connection with the continent of Europe, and became part of a great and powerful realm. Travel between England and the Continent was, among the rulers, probably more frequent than in many later centuries. The Crusades, of course, meant a great deal of coming and going.

During the course of the twelfth century, conditions in England were often desperately unsettled; but we can assume that, in spite of this, the everyday folk went on with their work and did their best to till the land and to make life comfortable for themselves and their children. With the very rudimentary means of communication, the effects of strife were localised; and barons might be waging a fierce struggle round a castle while a few miles away people were going on with their ordinary lives. Each hamlet and manor had largely to work as a self-contained and self-supplying unit.

CLOTHES AND ARMOUR

The moment has come, however, to get some idea of what the Normans looked like; and fig. *1* is drawn from details in the Bayeux Tapestry and other sources.

Starting on the left-hand side of the picture, the first figure is a Norman knight. On his head he has a conical iron helmet with the nose-piece that is characteristic of this period. His coat of mail was called a *hauberk*, and was made of leather, or a rough, strong linen, on which were sewn flat rings of iron. It was slit at the bottom to be more comfortable on horseback. Under the hauberk was worn a long tunic of linen, or wool, with sleeves to the wrist. The legs were covered with thick stockings, or trousers with feet, called *chausses*; and these were not knitted, but made of cloth, and cross-gartered with leather thongs. The shield was of metal, reaching as high as a man's shoulder, with a rounded top and pointed base.

The second figure is a Norman noble. He has an under-tunic of fine linen, or wool, above which he wears an over-tunic without sleeves, open at the sides, and fastened round the waist with a belt. His cloak is secured at the shoulder by being drawn through a ring brooch and knotted. He wears *chausses* and leather shoes like the knight. The Normans cut their hair short and were clean-shaven, and some also shaved the backs of their heads.

The lady has her hair done in two long plaits, and her head is covered with a small round veil, held in place by a metal circlet. Her under-tunic is of wool, or linen, like that of a man, with sleeves to the wrist. The *bliaut*, or over-tunic, fitted closely to the hip, from which it flowed out freely; it was laced at the sides, and cut low at the neck to show the garment beneath. She wears a jewelled belt, passed twice round the waist, and knotted in front. Her cloak is semicircular in shape, and fastened across the front with a cord.

25

The fourth figure is a man-at-arms. He wears a hauberk made of thick linen, or leather, covered with bands of leather fastened with metal studs, and beneath this an under-tunic. The helmet is carried under the arm, and it will be noticed that the hauberk has a hood with a leather cap-piece covering the head, to make the helmet more comfortable. He carries a lance and pennon. His *chausses* are cross-gartered, and the shoes are of leather.

The fifth figure has a hauberk made of overlapping pieces of thin metal sewn on to leather, or some thick material. His cloak is the same type as that of the noble; cloaks were only worn by people of the richer class.

The figure on the right-hand side of the picture is a bowman, who wears a soft felt cap of any colour except yellow, a colour worn only by the Jews. His stuff tunic is fastened at the waist by a belt of folded material, and his knickers are very wide, and made to unfasten down the side seams.

It will be noticed that the colours worn during the Norman period were rather dull in tone, and not nearly so gay as they became at a later period. Both the knight and the man-at-arms wear spurs. William depended largely on his cavalry; and the Bayeux Tapestry shows boat-loads of horses coming across the Channel.

The old method of fighting had been face to face, with a wall of shields, over which the soldiers hacked at one another. At the Battle of Hastings William employed archers, but the Saxons stood firm. The Normans then pretended to flee, which tempted Harold to break his line; and, when this happened, William's mounted knights rode through the gaps and threw Harold's army into confusion. The Bayeux Tapestry shows the Norman knight and bowman opposed to the Anglo-Saxon with his two-handed axe.

THE NORMAN NAVY

In the Bayeux Tapestry, again, we can examine the construction of William's ships. The Tapestry is supposed to have been worked by Queen Matilda and her ladies, who must have been wonderfully observant, for they show us, among other things, how the fleet was launched and navigated. At Oslo, Norway, there is an old ship, discovered in 1880 near Sandefjord.

5   A Norman Ship. (*Based on the Bayeux Tapestry*)

She dates in all probability from about A.D. 900, and was found buried in a mound, 18 feet above sea-level, with her prow pointing seaward. The length over-all is 79 feet 4 inches; beam, $16\frac{1}{2}$ feet; depth amidships, 6 feet; her gunwale above water, 2 feet 11 inches amidships, but 6 feet 6 inches at bow and stern. She is beautifully modelled under water, and is really more scientifically designed than some of the ships of later ages. A model was made at the end of the nineteenth century, and sailed across the Atlantic; so there is no doubt that these were sea-worthy boats. They were clinker-built—that is, of planks over-lapping at the edges. The boat at Oslo, presumably used as a Viking's burial-place, is known as the Gokstad ship, and there is a model of her in the Science Museum at South Kensington (see fig. 44 in *Everyday Life in Anglo-Saxon Times*). Between this model and the beautiful coloured figures of the Bayeux Tapestry we can get a very fair idea of the appearance of William's navy(5).

From their Norse ancestors, who built the Gokstad ship, the Normans inherited the art of seamanship. Their long, open boats had one mast and square sail, and oars were used when necessary. Shields were hung along the sides, and served as a protection to the rowers. The boat was steered by a large oar, secured in a loop of rope on the right; the word 'starboard', denoting the right of the vessel, is derived from the fact that the steer-board, or oar, was placed on that side. The end of the steering oar could be pulled up by a rope to avoid damage when grounding on a beach. There were no cabins, but a tent was stretched across at night, or during bad weather. The rowing benches were at the sides, with a centre gangway.

CASTLES AND CASTLE-BUILDERS

Having found out what the Normans did before they invaded England, what they looked like, and the boats they came in, we must next consider how they went to work when they had conquered the country.

William, only a few months after the battle of Hastings, had gone back to Normandy, leaving his half-brother Odo, Bishop of Bayeux, and his minister, William Fitz-Osbern, to take charge of affairs. It was this Odo who later conspired against William, and, having been arrested, was kept a prisoner until his brother's death.

The country was apparently peaceful, but, with the Conqueror away, risings broke out, and not until 1068 was it really subdued. The most important outbreak was at York, where 3,000 Normans were slaughtered and Swein, the King of Denmark, came to the assistance of the rebels. William bought off the Danes, and then proceeded to take terrible vengeance on the Saxons, and destroyed the whole countryside. He met with the most determined resistance in the Fen country around Ely, and Kingsley's *Hereward the Wake* contains a splendid description of the Saxons' last fight.

It was to hold the country in check that William started building castles. The Tower of London, Colchester in Essex, and the keeps of Chepstow, Pevensey, and possibly Bramber, date from about this time, and were built in stone. One can imagine the consternation of the Saxons as these gloomy piles of masonry began to rise, so forbidding and so unlike anything to which they had been accustomed. Later, we shall discuss wooden castles.

It must be remembered that the castle was supposed to belong to the king, and was erected only with his permission. William's early experiences with his barons in Normandy made him anxious not to allow them to become too powerful in

28

England. One of the causes of the anarchy of Stephen's reign was that permission to build new castles had been granted far too readily.

Before describing the Norman castle, it may be as well to give a few notes on the many varying types of fortifications that preceded it.

To discover the origins of fortification we must go right back to the New Stone Age. When men began to keep flocks and herds, they needed places where they could be secure from wolves and from the raids of neighbouring tribes. Hence the hill camps that were constructed on the chalk downs.

In the Bronze and Early Iron Ages, these were developed into wonderful strongholds, like Maiden Castle, near Dorchester.

At the end of the Early Iron Age, men had retreated to the swamps around Glastonbury, where they built a lake village, and made themselves secure behind a palisaded fence surrounded by water. We deal with the development of fortification up to this time in our book on the New Stone, Bronze, and Early Iron Ages, Vol. II of the "Everyday Life" Series. In Vol. III we show how the Romans, between A.D. 43 and 410, planned their cities, and stations, and walled them for defence, and how they built a Great Wall across the North of England to keep out the Picts.

When the Anglo-Saxons arrived in 449, they were content to sack the Romano-British cities, and built their own halls in the open country, where they could farm. Their idea of fortification consisted of not much more than a ditch and bank, with a palisaded fence on the top of the bank.

The later Vikings always liked to have water somewhere near them; so we find that their five strongholds, or burgs, were Lincoln on the River Witham, Stamford on the Welland, Leicester on the Soar, Derby on the Derwent, and Nottingham on the Trent.

Now we return to Norman times. On page 28 we noted that William, at an early date, started building stone castles. He was familiar with the Château d'Arques, near Dieppe, in Normandy, which was built by Guillaume d'Arques, in 1040, and has a stone keep, curtain walls, and gatehouse, and is altogether a wonderful piece of military architecture. It was here that, as a result of a quarrel, William besieged Guillaume d'Arques, his uncle; and most certainly he was not the man to see Château d'Arques, and then build wooden castles, like those shown on the Bayeux Tapestry, except for some good reason. The reason, of course, was that the timber castle could be erected very quickly; as William penetrated the country, he could easily throw one up, and leave a garrison in it to hold the inhabitants of the countryside in check, until it was decided that a more permanent building would be required.

We are told that William actually brought over with him from Normandy the timbers to make a fort; these were all framed and fitted beforehand, and the pins to fix them were packed in barrels.

These forts were built on the top of a high mound, or mount, so that the sentries could keep watch over a wide area. At the foot of the mount was a large enclosed yard, or bailey, where the garrison could keep their stores, with stables for the horses and cattle, and so on. This is the motte-and-bailey type of the Bayeux Tapestry; and we give a reconstruction of it in fig. 66 of Vol. IV of the "Everyday Life" Series.

In the shell type which followed, as at Berkhamsted, Lewes, and Arundel, the timber fort on the mount was replaced by a stone building, with stone walls to the bailey instead of the palisaded fence, which type we show in fig. 67, Vol. IV, "Everyday Life" Series.

We can now pass to a consideration of a typical twelfth-century castle; and, as an example, we have selected Castle Hedingham in Essex. This was built about 1130, and it closely resembles Rochester Castle erected about the same time. Fig. 6 gives some idea of how Hedingham looked originally. The castle stands to the north-east of the village on the edge of a hill which was cut, or scarped, to give the earthworks their shape. The old military architects were skilful at selecting sites for their castles that would render them dominating without too great an expense of labour. They did not raise an artificial mount if they could find a suitable hill.

The entrance to the Outer Bailey at Hedingham seems to have been on the south side. Here there was a gatehouse with its drawbridge and passage through. On either side were little chambers for the guard, and a staircase that led up to a room over the gate, from which the portcullis was worked. This was arranged so that it could be wound up or let down, and the

30

A · INNER BAILEY ON MOUNT
B KEEP BUILT ABOUT 1130-40.
C OUTER BAILEY
C.H.Q.

6   Bird's-eye View of Castle Hedingham, Essex.
(Partial reconstruction)

gateway below could be defended by bowmen shooting through
the embrasures of the battlements on the walls. In addition to
the portcullis, there were strong oak doors to the entrance
gateway. The gatehouse led directly into the bailey. Here were
the stables and granary, the barracks for the soldiers, and all
the many other workshops that must have been necessary.
There were then no shops just "round the corner"; so if arms
needed mending, or making, it had to be done within the
castle walls. Altogether, including squires, pages, servants, and
garrison, these castles must have housed a considerable number
of people. The bailey was surrounded by stone walls, called
curtain walls, with a ditch outside, and these were probably
flanked by projecting towers, which enabled the defenders to
shoot along the outside of the wall, and so keep off besiegers.

From the Outer Bailey we pass to the Inner Bailey, A, on the
mount, across a ditch spanned by a bridge, with another drawbridge before a second gateway. The Inner Bailey was circled
by walls with a ditch and bank outside. On the far side of the
ditch was planted a wooden palisade, so that the enemy had to
climb up the hill to the castle, then over the palisade, and so
down into the ditch, only to find that there was still the castle
wall to scale.

Very little is known of the appearance of the curtain walls and
bailey of a twelfth-century castle, because, though many of the

7 The Keep at Castle Hedingham, Essex; The Turrets restored,
and the Forebuilding reconstructed

keeps and gatehouses remain, the walls have generally been
altered many times since, to bring them up to date with the
military science of different periods, or have been pulled down
for the sake of the stone.

Parts of twelfth-century walls remaining at Berkhamsted show
that there were semicircular bastions projecting (6).

Fig. 7 shows the outside of the keep, which is the especial
glory of Hedingham. The walls, from 10 to 12 feet thick, were

32

built of flint concrete, faced with fine Barnack stone, and they rise up sheer, like grey cliffs, without a moulding or ornament to break the surface. Many modern architects tell us that architecture should be functional: that it should be designed, like a dynamo or aeroplane, to do its job, and that it can only be good in so far as it fulfils its function. Judged by this standard, Hedingham is as modern as any functional building now being built in France and Holland, Sweden or Germany. Indeed, we think it is a better example of the use of concrete than many a modern building. Concrete is really a rather unattractive building material, and depends for its form on the mould into which it is cast. This is called shuttering, and is made by the carpenter, and it is very costly. At Hedingham the Barnack stone facing takes the place of the shuttering and keeps the humble concrete in its proper place.

The only entrance to the keep was the one shown in the front of the forebuilding, and no more than the foundations of this remain at Hedingham. The forebuilding at Castle Rising in Norfolk is in a fine state of preservation, and shows that it was built to cover in a staircase leading up to an outer vestibule. From this, at Hedingham, one turned to the right, and entered the keep proper through another door protected by a portcullis, on what we should now call the first floor. The ground floor below was reached by going down the circular staircase inside the keep.

It might be as well to refer now to the plan (*8*). This shows the great hall on the second floor; but all the floors were very much the same. A large central room is lighted by windows recessed in the wall(*9*).

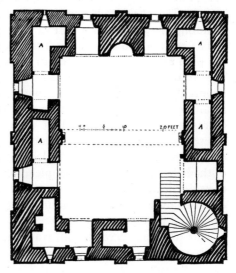

8   Plan of the Keep at Hedingham

33

Windows become broader as they rise in the buildings; for, during a siege, the windows above were less likely to be dangerous than the windows beneath. In the thickness of the walls are small chambers at A, A. The rooms on the first, second, and third floors have fireplaces. The *garderobes*, or lavatories, were placed in the angle opposite the stairs, and it should be noted that they are cut off by a lobby ventilated by a window. The medieval garderobe was just a shaft in the thickness of the wall, and must have been rather noisome.

The ground floor was probably used as a storehouse, and the wall chambers as dungeons. The first, or entrance, floor was a guard-room. The great hall over was the general living-place, and the floor above may have been the bower for the women. The well of the castle was in the keep, so that the garrison could be sure of water in a siege.

The staircase was in one of the angles, and led up to a square tower opening on to the battlements, with similar towers at the other three angles of the castle. Here the guard did sentry-go, 75 feet above the level of the top of the mount. Thus they could see a long way over the trees, and prevent surprise by the enemy.

Fig. *9* shows the interior of the great hall. In the average keep, like the one we have drawn, this was a room about 39 feet long by 31 feet wide; but in the larger castles, like the Tower of London, there are rooms 95 feet long by 40 feet wide.

The entrance to one of the little rooms, which are shown on the plan at A, A, can be seen in the drawing of the great hall, just above the two hounds held by the huntsman. The little rooms did not always have separate windows; and the only means of light and ventilation was then the opening at the entrance, probably covered at night with a leather curtain. These rooms were used as bedchambers by the principal members of the family, the serving-men sleeping in the rushes on the floor of the hall. In the daytime people lived much more together than they do nowadays; and, if we could return to the days when Hedingham was built, we should probably be astonished by the noise and by the lack of privacy.

This drawing serves to illustrate the first great problem that the Normans and other early builders had to contend with: how to roof over a large space. At each side of the fireplace are recesses in the thickness of the wall with a window at the end, and it will be noticed that they have a top to them like a small railway tunnel; there is a semi- or half-circular arch in front, and the line of this is carried through. This is what is known as a barrel vault, and it was the earliest method of roofing in stone. The stones of the arch in front are wedge-shaped and so cannot fall out, and are known as *voussoirs*, and a barrel vault is like many arches placed one behind the other. It is a feature we must understand; for, later on, the builders found that, by making one vault cut across another, all sorts of beautiful effects could be obtained. The fan vaulting of Henry VII's Chapel

9   The Great Hall at Hedingham ("Norman" style)

at Westminster Abbey(*168*) is a development of our barrel vault.

The Normans could build a vault across a small space, but did not know how to do it over a large room, so this great hall shares some of the characteristics of most Norman cathedrals. In the castle, the little rooms are vaulted in stone, but the hall has a beamed ceiling. In the cathedral, the side aisles are vaulted and the nave has a timber roof.

Now let us examine the nature of the difficulty that confronted the Norman builders of this great hall, its size being 39 feet long by 31 feet wide. Their first idea, perhaps, was to throw beams across the narrowest space—that is to say, across the width. But this would have meant that the beams used would have had to be at least 34 feet long, to give a bearing on the walls at each end. There were plenty of forests in the twelfth century, but there were not any circular-saws, and all beams and boards and planks had to be cut out of the trees by hand, a long and laborious business. Therefore the old builders economised in timber. What they did in the case of this hall was to build the very beautiful arch across the width, which enabled them to place the beams lengthways. The timbers they employed did not need to be longer than about 20 feet, because one end rested on the main wall and the other on the arch. Such beams would be easy to obtain. Across them came the smaller joists of the floor above.

So the arch was put in because it was a constructional necessity, and while they were doing it the old builders made it beautiful; which, if you come to think about it, is not at all a bad rule. From our point of view this little problem is worth consideration, because, as we jog along through the centuries, we shall always be running up against it, or against similar problems that have been overcome, and always in a pleasant way.

The windows of the great hall were very narrow, and of course did not have any glass; at night, or when the weather was very bad, they were closed by wooden shutters; but during the daytime the wind must have blown through, and the draughts and smoke made what we should consider a very uncomfortable house.

The fireplace, built on an outside wall, had what is called a flue, or escape, for the smoke; but this, instead of going up and finishing above the roof level in a chimney-stack, as flues do nowadays, was carried at an angle through the thickness of the wall, and came out into the open air behind one of the buttresses.

The gallery, which runs round the whole hall, was reached from the staircase in the angle turret. The gallery is contrived in the thickness of the wall, and so takes up the space used for the little rooms on the other floors. It is a very beautiful feature, and adds greatly to the hall's appearance.

FURNITURE AND FOOD

The furniture of this period was very simple, and consisted of tables, on trestles, and benches rather like school forms; there would have been one or two heavy chairs, or seats, and the floor was strewn with rushes. Meals were served in the great hall, and cooking is supposed to have been done in a kitchen in the bailey; but it is difficult to see how, in these conditions, the food carried such a distance on winter days could have remained eatable. In a manuscript of the early part of the twelfth century there is an illustration of a Norman butler in his office, which shows his assistants carrying food up an inside ladder, or staircase. The large room on the first, or entrance, floor was no doubt used for cooking, besides serving as a guard-room; the plan of this floor is just the same as the great hall over—it has a fireplace and chambers in the thickness of the wall, so there was plenty of room for both purposes, and during ordinary times it would not have been necessary to maintain a large guard inside the keep.

In the Bayeux Tapestry, Norman cooks are shown boiling a pot over one fire, and roasting at another, and then serving dinner through a doorway into the hall, and carrying the food in upon the spits on which it had been roasting (10).

Musicians often preceded the servants, and played while the meat was being served; harpers came and recited romances. Minstrelsy was in high repute among the Normans; the king had a minstrel, and every

10   Serving Food on Spits.
(*From the Bayeux Tapestry*)

11 Jugglers

gentleman of position maintained one, or more, as part of his household. Bands of acrobats and tumblers came to give displays.

Before we leave the Norman great hall, attention should be drawn to the zigzag ornament round the arches. The design is called the *chevron* pattern, and, like the slender columns in the angles, is a sign of Norman work.

The drawing(*12*) shows the circular staircase in the angle tower of the keep. This was all built in stone, and a tumble downstairs must have been a painful experience. Each step had a circular piece worked on it at one end, and at the other was long enough to be built into the wall; the front edge of one step was laid on the back edge of the one below, and the circular piece in the centre fitted exactly over the one underneath, and in this way formed the central stone column, or newel. For a long time most staircases were like this one.

MANORS AND GRANGES

The nobles who inhabited the Norman castles probably had their manor-houses too, just as the convents had granges on their outlying estates. In Jocelin of Brakelond's *Chronicle*, a wonderful manuscript of the twelfth century, we read how Abbot Samson narrowly escaped being burned to death in

12 The Staircase at Hedingham

1182, when staying at one of his granges, the only door of the upper storey of the house being locked, and the windows too narrow to admit escape. This sounds as if the abbot were in the solar of a house rather like that illustrated in fig. 72, and which by that time had become typical of the thirteenth century. It is to these granges that we must look if we are to understand how houses became more comfortable and less castle-like. Courageous indeed would have been the baron who dared molest Abbot Samson, a priest capable of bearding Cœur-de-Lion himself. The Church was strong; and, when the monastic granges were planned, it was not so necessary to consider defence, and comfort could be studied. The monks appear to have followed a much older building tradition than that of the Norman Castle.

In Vol. IV of our "Everyday Life" Series, we suggested

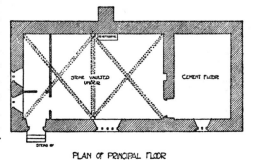

PLAN OF PRINCIPAL FLOOR

13 Boothby Pagnell Manor-House, Lincolnshire. (*From drawings by Sydney R. Jones*)

39

that the Anglo-Saxon hall, described in *Beowulf*, was rather like a glorified aisled barn, and this hall remained the central feature of the English house until the time of Elizabeth. When the monks planned their granges, they followed the old Anglo-Saxon buildings, and we find the same idea in the living part of their monasteries. See plan(*15*). The monks' warming room was in the same position as the cellar with the solar over it; the hall suggested the refectory, and the kitchen and offices kept the same position.

The nobles, when visiting an abbot and staying at one of his granges, would be struck by the greater convenience and comfort of such a house, and so follow it when building their manor-houses, only adding more defensive works.

The manor-house at Boothby Pagnell in Lincolnshire is a happy survival of a small twelfth-century manor-house(*13*). The heiress of the Boothbys married one of the Pagnell family from Newport Pagnell in Buckinghamshire. The arrangement is typical: a vaulted lower storey used as a cellar, without any connection with the upper living floor, which is reached by an outside stair. There are pleasant windows, and fireplaces on both floors connecting with a large chimney.

We also find that halls were built inside the curtain-walls of the castles in addition to the keeps. This was the origin of what is now called the Norman House at Christchurch, Hampshire, built between 1125 and 1150.

Whereas the hall described in *Beowulf* was obviously on the ground floor, Harold in the Bayeux Tapestry is shown dining in a hall raised up to the first floor on a vaulted undercroft, with stairs leading up to the hall outside. This plan, which was adopted at Christchurch, made it possible to have larger windows to the hall than if it had been on the ground floor. There appears to have been a kitchen at one end of the hall and a tower for the garderobes, and that is all. We illustrated this Christchurch house in Vol. IV of the "Everyday Life" Series, and we recommend our readers to go and see it.

TOWN-LIFE: A PICTURE OF LONDON

So far as the towns were concerned, there is an amusing and graphic picture of London and its work and play written by Fitzstephen, who "lived in the reign of King *Stephen*, wrote in the Reign of *Henry the Second*, and deceased in 1191, in the Reign of *Richard the First*". We give a few extracts:

A Description of the most honourable City of London

The Situation thereof. Amongst the noble Cities of the World, honoured by Fame, the City of *London* is the one principal Seat of the Kingdom of *England*, whose Renown is spread abroad very far; but she transporteth her Wares and Commodities much farther, and advanceth her Head so much the higher. Happy she is in the Wholesomeness of the Air, in the *Christian* Religion, her Munition also and Strength, the Nature of her Situation, the Honour of her Citizens, the Chastity of her *Matrons*; very plentiful also in her Sports and Pastimes, and replenished with honourable Personages. All which I think meet severally to consider.

The Temperateness of the Air. In this Place, the Calmness of the Air doth mollify Men's Minds, not corrupting them with Lusts, but preserving them from savage and rude Behaviour, and seasoning their Inclinations with a more kind and free Temper.

On the Strength and Scite of the City. It hath on the east Part a Tower Palatine, very large and very strong; whose Court and Walls rise up from a deep Foundation: The Mortar is tempered with the Blood of Beasts. On the West are two Castles well fenced. The Wall of the City is high and great, continued with seven Gates, which are made double, and on the North distinguished with Turrets by Spaces. Likewise on the South *London* hath been inclosed with Walls and Towers, but the large River of *Thames*, well stored with Fish, and in which the Tide ebbs and flows, by Continuance of Time, hath washed, worn away, and cast down those Walls. Farther, above in the west Part, the King's Palace is eminently seated upon the River; an incomparable Building, having a Wall before it, and some Bulwarks: It is two Miles from the City, continued with a Suburb full of People.

Of the Gardens planted. Every-where without the Houses of the Suburbs, the Citizens have Gardens and Orchards planted with Trees, large, beautiful, and one joining to another.

Of their Pastures. On the north Side are Fields for Pasture, and open Meadows, very pleasant; among which the River Waters do flow, and the Wheels of the Mills are turned about with a delightful Noise. Very near lieth a large Forest, in which are woody Groves of wild Beasts; in the Coverts whereof do lurk Bucks and Does, wild Boars and Bulls.

Of the Fields. The arable Lands are no hungry Pieces of Gravel

41

Ground; but like the rich Fields of *Asia*, which bring plentiful Corn, and fill the Barns of those that till them with a dainty Crop of the Fruits of *Ceres*.

Of their Wells. There are also about London, on the North of the Suburbs, choice Fountains of Water, sweet, wholesome, and clear, streaming forth among the glistening Pebble-stones: In this Number, *Holy well*, *Clerken-well*, and Saint *Clements'-well*, are of most Note, and frequented above the rest, when Scholars and the Youth of the City take the Air abroad in the Summer Evenings.

A good City, when it hath a good Lord.

How the Affairs of the City are disposed. . . . there is in *London* upon the River's Bank a public Place of Cookery, among the Wines to be sold in the Ships, and in the Wine Cellars. There every Day you may call for any Dish of Meat, roast, fried, or boiled; Fish both small and great; ordinary Flesh for the poorer Sort, and more dainty for the Rich, as Venison and Fowl . . .

Of Smithfield. Without one of the Gates is a certain Field, plain [or smooth] both in Name and Situation. Every *Friday*, except some greater Festival come in the Way, there is a brave Sight of gallant Horses to be sold: Many come out of the City to buy or look on, to wit, Earls, Barons, Knights, Citizens, all resorting thither. It is a pleasant Sight there to behold the Nags, well fleshed, sleek and shining, delightfully walking . . .

The Pests of LONDON. The only Plagues of *London* are immoderate Drinking of idle Fellows, and often Fires.

Sea Fights. In *Easter* Holidays they counterfeit a Sea Fight: A Pole is set up in the Middle of the River, with a Target well fastened thereon, and a young Man stands in a Boat which is rowed with Oars, and driven on with the Tide, who with his Spear hits the Target in his Passage; with which Blow, if he break the Spear and stand upright, so that he hold Footing, he hath his Desire; but, if his Spear continue unbroken by the Blow, he is tumbled into the Water, and his Boat passeth clear away . . .

Summer Sports. Upon the Holidays all Summer, the Youth is exercised in Leaping, Shooting, Wrestling, casting of Stones, and throwing of Javelins fitted with Loops for the Purpose, which they strive to fling beyond the Mark; they also use Bucklers, like fighting Men. As for the Maidens, they have their Exercise of Dancing and Tripping until Moon-light.

Sport upon the Ice. When that great Moor, which washeth *Moorfields*, at the north Wall of the City, is frozen over, great Companies of young Men go to sport upon the Ice; then fetching a Run, and setting their Feet at a Distance, and placing their

Bodies sidewise, they slide a great Way. Others take Heaps of Ice, as if it were great Mill-stones . . .

. . . Some are practised to the Ice, and bind to their Shoes Bones, as the Legs of some Beasts, and hold Stakes in their Hands, headed with Sharp Iron, which sometimes they strike against the Ice; and these Men go on with Speed, as doth a Bird in the Air, or Darts shot from some warlike Engine . . .

THE HOUSES OF THE PEOPLE

A good deal of information can be gathered from Building Regulations, issued in London in 1189, during the reign of Richard I. Houses before that time had been very generally built of wood, and roofed with thatch, and frequent conflagrations made the citizens decide that the time had come to adopt safety measures. Stone houses, covered with tiles, are therefore recommended. There are long descriptions of stone party-walls (those between the houses); they are to be 3 feet thick and 16 feet high, so the houses themselves could not have been very high, and apparently the rest of the house was still built of wood. The accommodation appears to have been a hall, or houseplace, on the ground floor, with perhaps a lean-to addition at the back for a kitchen, and the solar, or private room, a mere loft over the hall, lighted by a window in the gable at the front. These gables would naturally have come into being, as the roofs sloped down towards the party-wall at either side of the house.

A twelfth-century street, then, would have been made up of a series of rather low gables, side by side, the gutters between spouting water on to the pavements as often as the weather was wet. Some of the houses would have been higher than the others; for in these early by-laws of 1189 the householder is allowed to raise his half of the party-wall should he wish to do so.

In the country, the villeins' cottages would be much the same—a simple oblong building, with a houseplace, and perhaps a small shed, or kitchen, at one end, and a loft over. Again, before we describe such accommodation as very rough, we must remember that people were used to living in the open air, and, like sailors nowadays, only caught colds when they went indoors. For example, the monks had the best opportunity of being comfortable, yet they passed most of their time in the open cloisters. Some Norman street houses at Lincoln, one of them known as the Jews' House, are still lived in—an impressive record of eight hundred years' habitation.

THE CONQUEROR'S GOVERNMENT

Having studied the buildings he raised, we must next consider how William ruled. He was a great soldier and a great builder; but his true claim to greatness lies in the fact that he did what even the Danish Wars had not been able to do—bound the country together by the Feudal System.

William's followers were rewarded by large grants of land, belonging to the Anglo-Saxons who were slain at the battle of Hastings, and to others whose estates were confiscated; and these lands they held direct from the king, and in return were bound to supply so many soldiers at the king's call. Later on, subjects began to pay money instead of giving their services.

Not until the Conquest had England as a whole been supposed to belong to the king. The Saxons had always held the tribal belief that land belonged to the community; they held it by common consent, and fought for it when there was a common danger; but arousing them was a slow and difficult business, and the damage was often done before the defenders could be got ready. Harold, for example, had the greatest difficulty in assembling his troops; and this had always been the experience of the Anglo-Saxon kings. Feudalism, as interpreted by William, was now to supply a remedy.

Under the Saxons the land was divided up into *folk land*, which belonged to the people and consisted of what was left over after allotments had been made to the freemen, and *common land*, held by communities, but gradually becoming personal to a family if the dues and fines were paid, and then known as *heir land*. *Book land* generally consisted of grants to religious houses from the *folk land*.

Right down to the Norman Conquest we find customs similar to those introduced by the Saxons in the fifth century. The freeman was the freeholder. Tacitus, the Roman, said of the Saxons: "They live apart, each by himself, as woodside, plain, or fresh spring attracts him"; which does not mean that they were quite solitary, but that each holding was occupied by a family, and all the different generations of that family. The

44

holding had its common fields and grazing land, and the village itself was roughly fenced in. Each holding had its *folk moot*, a place where they met to frame their laws and customs. The headman of the village, or the chief, developed into the lord of the manor, and the chieftains became the kings.

The Danish Wars had the effect of bringing the scattered communities together, and introduced the beginnings of the Feudal System, and so we find that the freeman became the villein of the lord. Under Canute, the freeman somewhat regained his position, as the lords were dispossessed of their lands. William kept his hold on the land by making the Feudal System much more rigid.

It was first weakened in 1159, when the introduction of a Scutage Tax allowed the barons to pay the king a sum of money instead of following him to war. In Jocelin of Brakelond's *Chronicle* there is an interesting account of how this worked. The king calls on the abbot for the services of four knights to go to France, and give aid against the king there. The knights demur, saying that "neither had they, nor their fathers, ever gone out of England" for such a purpose; so the abbot goes to France instead, and offers money, which is not accepted, and in the end hires four mercenaries.

THE LIFE OF THE MONASTERY

The *Chronicle* of Jocelin of Brakelond brings us to a new aspect of everyday life in England during the twelfth century—the Monastery—the centre of all the civilising influences of the time. While nobles of the day hunted or fought, it was left to the Church to civilise, and the monastery attracted all those men who were anxious to do what we now call social work.

The Normans built not only castles but catherdals and monasteries too. Many of these still remain; both Norwich and Ely Cathedrals are largely Norman, and both were originally the churches of Benedictine monasteries. We shall have a good idea of religious life in those early days when we understand that what we now call a cathedral was then, in some cases, merely the private chapel of a convent; the cloisters and a few of the other buildings may remain, but what we now see is only a part of the original whole. This is explained by our plan(*13*).

Where the monastic church was used as a cathedral, it was

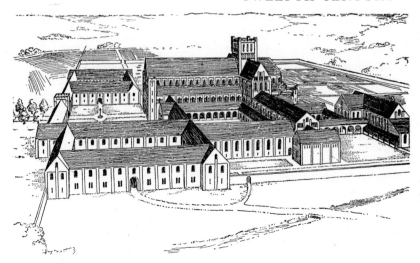

14 Exterior of a Benedictine Monastery

called a conventual cathedral; the bishop took the place of the abbot, and had the right to preside in the chapter-house. The prior and convent looked after the buildings, and continued to do so until the time of Henry VIII, when they were replaced by deans and chapters of secular canons. Cathedrals of the old foundation had deans and secular canons from the start.

Some of the terms, frequently used in later pages, are explained below:

A Cathedral is the bishop's church and the principal church in a diocese.

A Diocese is that part of the country over which the bishop rules.

A See means the seat of a bishop, or where his cathedral is.

The Parish originated with the holding of the lord, and his chaplain was the parish priest. The king's chaplains became the bishops.

A house for monks, by the way, is often referred to as a monastery, and a house for nuns as a convent. This is wrong. Convent is the term applied to the whole body either of monks or nuns, and monastery means only the actual group of buildings,

46

and it is used for the houses both of monks and of nuns, though the latter may also be called a nunnery.

Figs. *14* and *15* show a twelfth-century Benedictine monastery. One is a plan and the other a bird's-eye view, and the plan has numbers that correspond with those in the text, and will enable the uses of the various buildings to be followed. The top of each picture is the north, the right-hand side is the east, the left-hand the west, and the bottom the south. So, starting at the left-hand, or to the west, where 1 is marked, we enter by the gatehouse into the great court. Here all were free to come who had any business to do; and the court must have presented a busy scene, crowded with pilgrims, knights and men-at-arms, merchants and minstrels. There was a porter on duty at the gatehouse. At 2 was the almonry, where alms were given to the poor, and sometimes

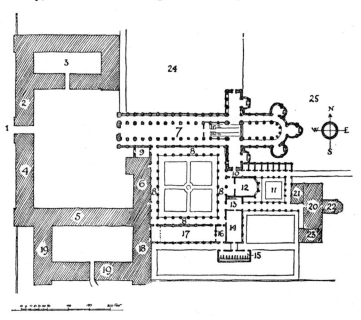

15   Plan of the Benedictine Monastery shown as fig. 14

1 The Gatehouse
2 The Almonry
3 Stables and granaries
4 Place for the poorer guests and pilgrims
5 Place for merchants, etc.
6 Abbott's or prior's lodge
7 Church
8 Cloister
9 Outer parlour
10 Slype or passage-way
11 Small coister
12 Chapter-house
13 Parlour
14 Stores or cellars
15 Lavatories
16 Warming-room
17 Refectory
18 Kitchens and offices
19 Bakehouse, Mill and Brew-house
20 Infirmary
21 Misericorde
22 Infirmary Chapel
23 Infirmary Kitchen
24 Cemetery
25 Gardens and fishponds

there was a school close by for poor children. At 3 were the stables and granaries. Here the horses of the guests and travellers were put up. It is doubtful if there were many inns in England where travellers could obtain food and lodging until the middle of the fourteenth century.

In the towns there were ale-houses, cook-shops, and hostelries; for, a little later, in the time of John, 1212, we read that, after a fire, "all ale-houses be forbidden except those licensed by the Common Council, and that no baker bake or ale-wife brew by night with reeds or straw, but wood only"; all cook-shops, moreover, were to be whitewashed.

It was part of the duty of monks to entertain strangers. Their accommodation was divided up: just south of the gate-house, at 4, was the place for the poorer guests and pilgrims; at 5 would be placed the merchants and like folk; and at 6 was the abbot's or prior's lodging, where nobles or the king would be entertained. Jocelin of Brakelond's *Chronicle* gives an idea of the great size of the twelfth-century monastery. He says that, after Abbot Samson's installation, "he retired to his chamber, spending his day of festival with more than a thousand dinner guests with great rejoicing".

Jocelin also gives a note of how guests were entertained:

When the abbot is at home, he is to receive all guests of what-soever condition they may be, except religious and priests of secular habit, and except their men who present themselves at the gate of the court in the name of their masters; but if the abbot be not at home, then all guests of whatsoever condition are to be received by the cellarer up to thirteen horses. But if a layman or clerk shall come with more than thirteen horses, they shall be entertained by the servants of the abbot, either within the court-lodge, or without, at the expense of the abbot.

At 7 was the church, and the west door was generally placed opposite the gatehouse, so that on saints' days it could be opened for processions. The north door was used by the people when there were special services for them in the nave; but the monks used the choir, which extended into the nave.

At 8 was the cloister, a very important part of the monastery. When we go round a cathedral now, we are struck by the beauty of the vaulted walks, with the arched and traceried openings on the garth, or space, in the middle; but, when it was built, it

48

served not only as a corridor leading to the various parts of the building but also as a place where the monks spent a great part of their time. For this reason it was usually placed to the south of the church, so as to be on the sunny side.

The north walk, the one next to the church, was reserved for study, and little recesses called carrels were sometimes built on the side next to the garth, like small studies, where the monks could read their manuscripts. A drawing is given in our fifteenth-century chapter (*163*) showing these recesses, and fig. *79* one of the aumbries or cupboards in which manuscripts were kept.

The east walk was very much used, because it led to the chapter-house, the passage to the infirmary, and the refectory. It was in the east walk that the abbot washed the feet of thirteen poor men, representing Christ and the twelve Apostles, on the Thursday before Easter (Maundy Thursday).

The south walk was parallel with the refectory, and in the west walk were taught the novices. In some of the old cloisters, little figures used for playing games are cut in the stone benches.

At 9 was the outer parlour, where a porter sat who kept the cloister door, and here merchants could sell their wares, or monks receive visits from their relatives after the chapter.

At 10 was the slype, or passage-way, leading to the scriptorium, or place where the monks wrote their manuscripts. In these days before printing, all the church service books were made by hand and beautifully illuminated, and there must have been letter-writing as well to carry on the business of the convent. It was done in these little rooms, each of which had a window to the north, and a door opposite opening on to the north walk of the smaller cloister at 11.

At 12 was the chapter-house, or parliament of the convent.

At 13 was the parlour, or place where the monks could talk, and generally there were stairs leading up to the monks' dormitory above. This latter was a long upper chamber, which also connected with the south transept of the church, so that the monks could easily go there for services during the night.

At 14 were various stores and cellars.

At 15 were lavatories, in two stories, the upper communicating by a bridge with the south end of the monks' dormitory for use at night.

At 16 was the warming-room, where the monks could warm themselves, after service in the church on a cold winter's day; and in those days churches were not heated. The Romans had used elaborate heating systems here in England, seven or eight centuries before, but the methods they employed had long since been forgotten.

At 17 was the refectory, where they all fed; and near the door to the south walk of the cloister there was always a place where the monks could wash their hands, with a recess where the towels were kept.

At 18 were the kitchens and offices, opening out on to a courtyard, around which were grouped the bakehouse, mill, and brewhouse at 19.

At 20 was the infirmary, where sick monks could lie, and 21 was the misericorde, where such of them as needed it were allowed to eat meat. The infirmary had its own chapel at 22, and kitchen at 23.

The monks' cemetery was at 24, to the north of the church, and the gardens for growing vegetables, with the fish-ponds, were to the east, at 25. A site was selected which had a stream of good water, and this was diverted to form the fish-ponds, and then led on to various parts of the monastery, to take away the sewage, and turn the water-mill which ground the corn to make bread.

Our plan, of course, must not be regarded as an exact copy of any particular monastery. The Benedictines generally built on somewhat similar lines, but the positions of the various parts were often varied to suit local requirements. Thus, at Westminster Abbey, the outer parlour was at the west end of the south cloister walk.

Yet, broadly speaking, this is the layout of many twelfth-century monasteries. As time went on, the cloister, which perhaps had been built in wood at the start, was rebuilt, say during the fourteenth century, in stone, or the chapter-house was beautified. A central tower fell down, or there was a fire, and the parts destroyed were rebuilt in the style of the period.

At the dissolution of the monasteries, in Henry VIII's reign, the need for the monastic parts of the building passed away, and so they fell into disrepair, or were altered out of all recognition; but here and there parts remain. There are fine

16 Exterior of Orford Castle, Suffolk (the battlements restored)

17 The Chapel, at Orford Castle, Suffolk

18 (*Top*) The funeral procession of Edward the Confessor. The church on the left is the Saxon Westminster Abbey
19 Part of William's baggage train. A wine cart, and porters bearing suits of armour and weapons

remains of the domestic parts of the monasteries at Chester and Durham and elsewhere; but perhaps the most extensive are at Cleeve Abbey, near Washford, in Somerset, where the church has vanished. At Westminster Abbey, the boys of Westminster School use what was the old monks' dormitory as a schoolroom, and they have the abbot's hall, which at Westminster is on the west side of the west walk of the cloister, as a dining-hall. Lucky boys, to be taught in the shadow of that glorious abbey, and feed in the abbot's hall!

An idea of the size of the old monasteries may be gained by giving the dimensions of some of the parts. At Westminster the dormitory was 170 feet long, and the refectory was 130 feet long by 38 feet wide. The kitchen at Canterbury was 45 feet square, and at Worcester 35 feet. The guest-hall at Canterbury was 150 feet long by 40 feet wide.

Now for the constitution of the convent. At the head came the abbot, then the prior, who was his chief assistant. There was a sub-prior, and beneath him were the monks. The chantor, or precentor, acted as singer and librarian. The sacristan took care of the church and the buildings. The cellarer was the steward, who controlled all the business side. The hospitaller looked after the guests, and the infirmarer the sick, while the almoner distributed the alms. The master of the novices was responsible for their education.

The monks' day started at midnight, and the new day was ushered in with prayer. This first service was called Matins. The sub-sacristan rang a bell in the monks' dormitory, where they had gone to bed at half-past seven in the evening in the winter and half-past eight in the summer.

They descended directly into the church, by stairs from the dormitory, into the south transept. After a brief interval, Lauds commenced about one o'clock, and by half-past one or two all the monks were back in bed again.

They were roused at seven in the morning for Prime, which did not take very long, and was followed by an early Mass for the servants and workpeople, of whom there were a great number, and, while this was being celebrated, the monks washed and finished dressing.

Before the next Mass the monks had breakfast, of about ¼ lb. of bread and ⅓ pint of wine or beer. There was not any tea, coffee, or cocoa in the twelfth century, but there may sometimes have been porridge.

This next Mass preceded the daily chapter, held about nine o'clock. Here a junior monk, who was also the weekly reader in the refectory at meals, read out notices of the lives of the martyrs and saints who would be commemorated on the following day, and afterwards there was a discussion on the affairs of the house, seals were put to any documents, and any errring monks were punished.

With regard to discipline in the monastery, Jocelin gives us an interesting account of a mutiny of the monks, accustomed to the easy ways of Abbot Hugo, against the stricter rule of Samson, who goes away so that his anger may cool, and on his return says: "I would have taken vengeance on thee, had not I been angry." So they were punished, and then:

> On the morrow morning we decided on humbling ourselves before the abbot, by word and gesture, in order to mitigate his mind. And so accordingly was done. He, on the other side, replying with much humility, yet always alleging his own justice and turning the blame on us, when he saw that we were conquered, became himself conquered. And bursting into tears, he swore he had never grieved so much for anything in the world as for this, first on his own account, and then secondly and chiefly for the public scandal which had gone abroad, that St. Edmund's monks were going to kill their abbot.

To continue with the monks' day, the chapter finished about half-past nine, leaving half an hour for conversation in the cloister before High Mass at ten. During this interval the officials settled the business of the day; and it must be remembered that the convent had large estates which had to be managed. The monks were great builders and deserve credit for much of the advance which was made in contemporary arts and crafts.

Dinner followed at eleven, and lasted half an hour, the monks washing their hands before and after the meal; when this was finished, the junior monks and novices played games in the garden, and the elders slept for an hour. During the afternoon the monks worked. St. Benedict, when he founded the Order in the sixth century, expressly arranged that his monks should do manual labour, and thus keep their bodies healthy and strong.

They were industrious gardeners, growing vegetables and medicinal herbs.

Vespers were at five o'clock in the winter and six in the summer, and then supper followed; after came Collations and reading in the chapter-house, followed by a short interval in the cloister in the summer and the warming-house in the winter. At seven in the winter and eight in the summer came Compline, and half an hour later all would be in bed, until they were roused again at midnight for Matins.

This was the way the old monks passed their days; it was a very peaceful and well-ordered existence, and there is little wonder that it attracted the studious man. The real work that the monastic order did is still occasionally lost sight of. Sheltered by the cloister and protected by their vocation, they were able, in a rough-and-tumble age, to establish all the influences that were to civilise England. The nunneries for women were conducted on the same lines.

There is an interesting account in Jocelin of Brakelond's *Chronicle* of how the monks elected an abbot, and were helped to do so by King Henry II. Jocelin entered St. Edmundsbury in 1174, when the abbot was Hugo, who was a very old man. The convent under his rule had got badly into debt. The Jewish usurers, who had lent him money, charged enormous interest, and poor Abbot Hugo was distracted. He went on pilgrimage to Canterbury in 1180, but, being thrown from his mule near Rochester, dislocated his knee, and died as a result of the fever caused by the bruises; and, sad to relate, his servants plundered his apartments as soon as he was dead. The king placed an inspector over the monastery, and meanwhile collected the revenues, and it was not until 1182 that they could set about electing a new abbot. Six of the elders selected the names of three of

20   The Investiture of an Abbot

their own monks whom they considered suitable, writing them down in a document which was sealed. And then the prior and twelve monks set off with it to see the king at Waltham; they walked there, their frock-skirts looped over elbow. Whereupon the king called on them to nominate three and, this being already done, the seal was broken, and the names found to be Samson the sub-sacristan, Roger the cellarer, and Hugo the third prior. The king called for three other names; at which the prior was named as one, the sacristan as the second, and Dennis, apparently a monk, the third. With these nominations, the king asked for three from other convents, and so they gave the prior of St. Faith, a monk of St. Neots, and another of St. Albans, and there were then nine names. The king then said three names might be struck off, and so those of the three strangers went. The sacristan withdrew, and the king ordered two more names to be struck off, and then another, which meant that Hugo the third prior and the monk Dennis retired, leaving only Samson and the prior. The venerable Dennis made a speech "commending the persons of the prior and Samson, but always in the corner of his discourse brought Samson in"; and Samson it was who was elected, and returned as abbot to the monastery he had left as sub-sacristan. This meant that he ranked as a peer, was lord of the manor, and had "fifty knights under him".

For four years Samson worked hard paying off the usurers; but, as soon as this had been done, they were marched over the borders and bidden never to return.

THE MONASTIC ORDERS

The principal Monastic Order was that founded by St. Benedict in A.D. 529. To the three vows of obedience, poverty, and chastity, he added that of manual labour for seven hours each day. This kept the monks in good health and happy. The Benedictines were the largest Order, and celebrated for their learning. St. Augustine, the apostle of the Anglo-Saxons, was a Benedictine.

Our illustration (*14*) is of a Benedictine monastery.

The Carthusians had their principal monastery at the Charterhouse in London, which after the dissolution of the monasteries was reclaimed by Thomas Sutton and remodelled as the Charterhouse School.

A description of the life led in a Carthusian monastery and details of the buildings are given in the chapter on the fifteenth century. (See fig. *161*.)

The Cistercians, who were farmers, were largely responsible for bringing back into cultivation the districts in the north wasted by the Conquerer. They generally settled down in some very remote place, near a good river; and their buildings closely resembled those of the Benedictines, but are frequently a little later in architectural style. Because they were placed far from centres of population, their churches could not be used after the Dissolution as cathedrals or parish churches, and have fallen into ruin. Nevertheless they are lovely and pleasant even in decay, witness such piles as Fountains, Rievaulx and Byland in Yorkshire, with Tintern in the west and Beaulieu and Netley in the south.

The Augustinians were founded in the eleventh and twelfth centuries; and there were other Orders that we cannot mention here.

The monks founded hospitals at places of pilgrimage, and along the high roads, for the entertainment of poor pilgrims and travellers. Some were for lepers, others for poor and infirm persons, who were called bedesmen. St. Bartholomew's Hospital in London is a survival of a much older institution of this kind. As time went on, other people gathered round the monasteries, and so towns sprang up.

Finally, there were the Military Orders. The Knights of the Temple, or Templars, were founded under Augustinian rule at Jerusalem in 1118, between the first and second Crusades. They undertook the task of escorting pilgrims from the coast up to Jerusalem, protecting them from the infidel, against whom they waged war in defence of the Cross. In addition to these duties, the Templars took the usual vows of poverty, chastity, and obedience. The Order was founded in England by Stephen and the Temple Church in London enshrines their memory.

The Knights of St. John of Jerusalem, or the Knights Hospitallers, not originally a military Order, was founded in 1092 to afford hospitality to pilgrims to the Holy Land, and to care for the sick and wounded Crusaders. In the twelfth century they became military, and, with the Templars, maintained a standing army for the defence of Jerusalem. When Palestine was lost, they moved to Cyprus, then Rhodes, and finally Malta, where the buildings they erected still remain. They exercised a very useful influence in checking the Mohammedan invaders of Europe. The Hospitallers were introduced into England by Henry I, and founded houses here for novices to be trained in piety and military exercises.

The Trinitarians were founded in 1197 to rescue Christian captives, and were commonly called Mathurins.

THE MONASTIC INFLUENCE ON ARCHITECTURE

Having spoken of the various religious Orders, and more especially of the monastery and of the life that was led within its walls, we must say something about the part these Orders played in developing the architecture of the time; and here we shall find that their influence was very great indeed.

Fig. 21 shows the aisle of a monastic church, and the first point to which we wish to draw attention is the vaulted roof. In fig. 9 the plain barrel vaulting, designed to cover the recesses at each side of the fireplace, is particularly emphasised; and this was said to be like an ordinary railway tunnel. Now the vault to the aisle, illustrated here, shows the next development. There is the same barrel vault or railway tunnel along the aisle, but crossing it at right angles are other barrel vaults following the lines of the arches into the nave, and between each intersection so formed is a semicircular arch.

At the actual line of the intersection of the two semicircular barrel vaults an angle was formed, which was called the groin. Each bay of the vaulting, between the semicircular arches, was a square, and the line of the groin, if you were making a plan, would run diagonally across it. The first discovery the old builders made was that the actual elevation of the groin was that of an ellipse, or waggon-shaped, and this must be so because the groin springs or starts from the same line, and only rises to the same height as the arches crossing the aisle, which are semi-circular; and as its span is wider, because it goes across the diagonal of the bay, it must be of a flatter shape.

Now as to the way these early vaults were constructed. The semicircular arches across the aisle were built first; then rough wooden centres or moulds, of the shapes of the diagonal or groin, were put up, boards were laid on the top, and the vault

21   The Aisle of a Monastic Church, based on the
Norman work at Ely

was constructed in what is called rubble, rough stones, not yet
shaped as to the arches. When this was set, the centering was
taken down, and the vault was plastered on its underside. The
old builders had learned that the vault looked rather dumpy
because the groins were flatter than semicircles; next, that the

centre or crown of the vault was too flat, and the stones were inclined to fall out, and this also applied to the groins themselves.

So they proceeded to make the profile or true elevation of the groin semicircular—a step that raised the crown of the vault considerably above the tops of the semicircular arches crossing the aisle; and, to remedy this, the latter were taken up straight for the necessary distance, and then made semicircular as before. This was called stilting. But here another difficulty was encountered: the now semicircular groins, and the stilted crossing arches, all sprang or started from the same level, but the groins at once started curving away, because they were true semicircles, whereas the stilted arches went up straight for a foot or so. This was found to be ugly, because it made the crossing arches look as if they had been pushed in at the bottom between the two groins; a good example is to be seen in the chancel of Hemel Hempstead Church, Herts, illustrated in fig. 79, Vol. IV, "Everyday Life" Series, *Anglo-Saxon and Norman Times*. A further step was to spring all from the same level, but make the arches across the aisle pointed—the true solution of the problem; but it was not finally put into practice until the thirteenth century. The groin lines, too, were strengthened by the addition of stone ribs. Another surprise for the Norman builders was the discovery that, by crossing their vaults as described, they concentrated the thrust at particular points; and it became necessary to make their buttresses outside of more projection. The drawing shows the cushion-shaped capitals to the columns and other details characteristic of Norman work.

CHANGES IN CASTLE-BUILDING

Meanwhile military architecture, too, was changing and developing. After the accession of Henry II in 1154, which brought to an end the disastrous anarchy of the days of Stephen and Maud, England once again became part of a great European organisation. From A.D. 43 to, say, 410 we had been part of an empire that stretched across Europe from Babylon to Britain. At the end of the twelfth century, Henry II ruled all the land from the Pyrenees up through the western part of France; and Scotland, Ireland, and Wales were his vassals. Where the king's law ran, an Englishman was free to go, and return with new ideas and a fresh outlook on life. This is reflected in the everyday things. Hedingham, the subject of figs. *6* to *9*, built in 1130, is a typical Norman keep; but Orford, built by Henry II, and finished in 1167, shows some important differences.

To-day, the river Alde rises in the inward parts of Suffolk, and, having been joined by various tributaries, is a quite presentable stream by the time it has arrived at Snape. But at Aldeburgh, perhaps only two or three hundred yards from its destination, it changes its mind, direction, and name, and flows due south parallel with the sea, divided from it by a great shingle bank, to reach the ocean at last, twelve miles away at Shingle Street. In this last stage it is called Orr, and here from the earliest times has stood the pleasant little town of Orford, which, in the time of Henry, must have been an important trading centre.

We must now examine the plan of Orford(*22*). The first consideration of the designer seems to have been to get rid of the blind angle that occurred in the square keep, as at Hedingham. In fig. *8*, it is obvious that there was an area at the angles that the archers on the battlements could not reach without exposing themselves; but at Orford, by adopting a polygonal shape for the keep, with the three turrets as projecting bastions, the builders allowed no part of the walls to remain out of observation from the battlements above.

Fig. *16* illustrates the exterior of Orford. As at Hedingham, the entrance to the keep was on the first-floor level. The stairs up, shown on the sketch, are modern but probably on the old lines. The entrance was defended by a portcullis, in front of a stout oak door. It leads into the porter's lodge, with a dungeon beneath. Two more doors had to be passed to get into the

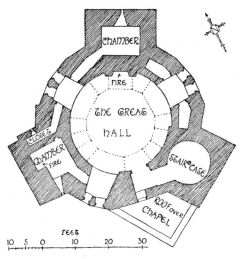

22 Orford Castle, Suffolk

23   A Twelfth-Century Kitchen Sink at Orford Castle, Suffolk

guard-room; and the staircase, in one turret, was only reached by going through the guard-room. This fine room had three windows like those shown in fig. *25*, with a chamber in one turret and the kitchen in another.

It is here that we find the twelfth-century sink (*23*), with its ingenious drain through the thickness of the wall to spout outside. Fig. *24* is the type of jug that would have been washed there.

Underneath the guard-room on the ground-floor level, but only reached by going down the staircase, was the

24   A Ewer found in Fenchurch Street, London, probably Twelfth Century. (*British Museum*)

25 Orford Castle, Suffolk: The Great Hall. The Gallery restored

great store-room of the castle, and in the centre, the well, so that the water-supply was secure in time of siege. The great hall (22, 25) was on what we should call the second floor, over the guard-room on the first; and the plan shows how cunningly the chambers and smaller recesses were contrived in the thickness of the walls.

Now we come to one of the most interesting details of Orford. The guard-room and the great hall are two noble rooms, the first some 22 feet high, the second nearly 27 feet. It is obvious that the small chambers in the turrets did not need to be so high; and two were placed one over the other in the same height as the big rooms or, as we should say now, in a mezzanine. In the guard-room, a little staircase at the left-hand side of the fireplace leads up to a room for the Captain of the Guard in the north turret. Half-way up the stairs in the south turret, a passage in the thickness of the wall leads first to the chapel(*17*), built over the porter's lodge at the entrance, and then the passage-way is continued along to the west turret, where the priests' chamber, complete with garderobe and wardrobe, was placed.

The main staircase continues up to the battlements, where one of the turrets was used as a bakehouse; the ovens are still there; and in the other was a guard-room for the sentries keeping a look-out for hostile craft which might attempt to raid the port below. If, by any chance, you are not interested in architecture, and can't spare a thought for the great king who reigned over Western Europe, and if you don't care very much about his castle and its architect, then you will reap a reward (which you do not deserve) when you reach the battlements—one of the most beautiful views in Suffolk, across the marshes to the sea beyond.

Before we leave Orford, two points must be noted. First, that the keep was originally the centre of an elaborate scheme of curtain walls which have now disappeared. Secondly, that the keep is more completely a house under one roof than anything that followed it for many years.

26 Haircutting in the
Twelfth Century

COUNTRY LIFE

Leaving buildings, we turn to the details of country life in the twelfth century. Here we shall find that the Domesday Survey is an invaluable source of information; for not only does it give us an idea of how much land was cultivated, and how many people inhabited England in 1085, but it also tells us what they were doing. The Commissioners set themselves to find out "the name of the manor, who held it in the time of King Edward the Confessor and who held it now, how many hides there were in each manor, how many ploughs on the domain, how many men, how many villeins, how many cottars, how many bondsmen, how many freemen, how many socmen (freemen paying a fixed rent), how much wood, how much meadow, how much pasture; what mills, what fish-ponds—how much it was worth, and whether more could be got out of it than to-day".

An entry in Domesday Book may read somewhat as follows:

> The Land of William of Braiose. The land is of three ploughs. The whole extent of arable is three ploughlands, though it was only assessed at two hides. There is one in the domain (William manages one ploughland himself), and five villeins and cottars with two ploughs (there are two teams in the domain). There is a mill of 18 shillings-worth and a fishery of 50 pence-worth.

And so England was parcelled out, for the Conqueror to estimate the value of his spoil.

The land was measured by the hide, suling, or caracute which equalled about 120 of our acres. It was found that about 5,000,000 acres were cultivated; that there were about 300,000 families, with a population of 2,000,000. We read of 9,300 landowners and clergy, 12,000 freeholders, 23,000 socmen or yeomen, 109,000 villeins or copyholders, 90,000 cottars or small copyholders, 25,000 bondsmen or landless men.

The counties were divided into hundreds, and the hundreds into manors. The manors contained the demesne, or domain, which was the lord's own land, and the holding of the villeins, which averaged 30 acres, or a virgate or yardland. The cottars had perhaps a cottage and 5 acres. Now as to how all this worked. We must, if we wish to understand the twelfth century, forget all about the twentieth and its constant talk of money. In the twelfth, instead of paying rent in money, you rendered service. The lord held his land from the king on this condition—he had to promise to help the king, and be his man; and the same idea ran through the whole of the society of the time. Here are typical conditions on which a villein held land. In the

27 A Shepherd

spring he had to plough 4 acres for his lord; and each villein supplied two oxen for the lord's plough team for three days in the winter, three in the spring, and one in the summer. In addition, he must work three days a week on the lord's land, or pay a yearly toll of 2s. 1½d., a hen, and sixteen eggs. He must follow his lord to war, and sit in his court of justice, and uphold customs which were eventually to become laws. So, if he had his duties, he also had his rights; and we call him a copyholder, because the terms of his holding were copied into the Court Roll, and so long as he rendered service in accordance with them, he could not be turned out. It was not in the lord's interest to oppress his villeins any more than it would be to a modern farmer's advantage to ill-treat his horses. The two classes depended very much on one another, and continued to do so until the time of the Black Death, which altered the conditions of country life. It is usual to think of the villein as a miserable bondsman, whereas, in reality, he formed the backbone of the countryside, free on three days in the week to work on his own holding, owning cattle and doing well or badly according to whether he was lazy or indus-trious. He was tied to the land, and could not leave his manor, except with the lord's consent; but then, in all probability, it never entered his head to do so, unless he went to the wars in France, or on a pilgrimage. The lord was in much the same position under the Feudal System. The villein's condition, like that of the labourer, depended on his master. In Jocelin's *Chronicle* we read that

coming down from London through the forest, I inquired of an old woman whom we came up to, whose wood this was, and of what manor; who was the master, who the keeper? The old woman answered, the wood belonged to the new Abbot of St. Edmunds, was the manor of Harlow, and the keeper of it was one Arnald. How did he behave to the people of the manor? I asked further. She answered that he used to be a devil incarnate, an enemy of God, and a flayer of the peasant's skins—skinning them like live eels as the manner of some is; but that now he dreads the new abbot, knowing him to be a wise and sharp man, and so treats the people reasonably.

In times of peace the village was like one large farm—the common fields were ploughed, harrowed, sown, and reaped by the joint labours of all the villeins; and each of the latter's

66

28 A Plough. (*From the Bayeux Tapestry*)

holdings consisted of a strip, or strips, in the open fields. The Bayeux Tapestry (*18, 19*) not only deals with the military aspect of the Conquest but illustrates the occupations of the country-side. A ploughman is ploughing; then comes a man who scatters the seed broadcast, while another leads a horse-drawn harrow, and a boy scares the crows away by slinging stones at them. The whole group is very much like that shown in the Luttrell Psalter, which we shall use to illustrate agriculture in the fourteenth century, except that the plough is of the two-wheeled variety. It is drawn by an animal that suggests an ox, and appears to be harnessed like a horse, not yoked like an ox. Had the designer of the tapestry known we were going to attempt a restoration, as fig. *28*, he, or she, might have taken a little more trouble with the details. As it is, there is no doubt at all about the two wheels, or the coulter behind them which makes the vertical cut, and what appears to be a furrow board. The country must have looked very different then; for the fields were not enclosed with hedges, but divisions were made by leaving what were called baulks of turf. The woods were used for feeding swine; the cattle grazed on the common land, and were largely killed off in the late autumn, because what we now call root crops were not yet grown, and it was difficult to feed cattle in the winter. There were meadows for making hay; thirty-eight vineyards are mentioned in Domesday Book, and a good deal of wine was produced. Everybody kept bees to get honey for sweetening purposes—remember you could not buy pounds of sugar in those days. The peasants' food consisted of pigs' flesh, and domestic fowls, vegetables, fruit, eggs, and cheese, the latter sometimes made from ewes' milk. Meat was much eaten, and in the winter it was salted. But, as salt was difficult to obtain, it was probably not very well cured; and this accounts for the many skin diseases often confused with leprosy.

ABBOTS AS LANDLORDS

To return to the conditions of landholding, abbots were in the position of lords of the manor, and had tenants. In Jocelin of Brakelond's *Chronicle* we read how difficult the cellerarius found it to collect the "reaping silver", or penny, that each householder had to pay instead of giving his labour to cut down the convent grain. "Before the town was free all of them used to reap as serfs; the dwellings of knights and chaplains and of the servants of the court lodge being alone exempt from this payment."

The cellerarius gave up trying to get it from the richer folk, and distrained on the poorer by taking instead a stool, a kettle, or even the house door; and there was so much commotion that the reap silver was commuted. Thus the holders of the town fields had to catch 4,000 eels in the marshes of Lakenheath, and bring them to their landlords the monks; but they became lazy, and brought half the number, and sometimes none at all—one feels sorry for the townsmen, because the eels may not have been there to be caught, and are known for slippery customers. So a new arrangement was made—that, instead of the eels, each holder should pay a penny for so many acres; but this was found troublesome, because the fields were divided up among so many people; sometimes the cellarer got 27*d.*, and then again only 10¼*d.* Another rule was, that the townsmen should put their sheep in the convent's pens at night, for the sake of the manure; but naturally they preferred to improve their own land in this way. There was trouble also with the mill and market dues. All of

29   Bargaining with the fruitsellers

31 Mixing drugs and compounding potions

30 Extracting an arrow

33 Head operations

32 A patient is sternly admonished

MEDICAL PRACTICE AT THE END OF THE TWELFTH CENTURY. *From MS. 0.1.20, Trinity College, Cambridge*

34 Corn-cutting with sickles, tying into sheaves, gleaning, carrying
to the granary, digging, and sowing

FIELD WORK FROM A TWELFTH-CENTURY MANUSCRIPT

which shows how the people, who at first gathered round the monastery for the protection that it afforded, and the work they found to do, were gradually working their way to an independent position as a township, and commuting their service for money payments, or rent.

There is another interesting note in Jocelin's *Chronicle* on mills. These generally belonged to the lord, and the villeins took their corn to his mill, and had to pay in kind for the grinding. A Dean Herbert ventured to build a mill without the abbot's consent, and was ordered to take it down by the abbot, who said: "I tell thee, it will not be without damage to my mills; for the townsfolk will go to thy mill, and grind their corn at their own good pleasure; nor can I hinder them, since they are free men. I will allow no new mills on such principle." The abbot sent his men to take the mill down, who found that the dean had forestalled them, so that he might not lose the timber.

TRADE AND TRAVEL

So far as food was concerned, the average twelfth-century manor was very nearly self-supporting; but goods could be exchanged at the local markets, and luxuries were obtained at the great fairs. The fair at Stourbridge, near Cambridge, lasted from September 18 to October 9, and merchants came to it from places as far away as Bruges and Hamburg, Bordeaux and Rouen, and the Italian cities. Here could be brought foreign wines, furs from the Baltic, Flemish cloth and lace, salt and spices, and the farmers could dispose of their cattle, hides, and wool.

The Crusades and pilgrimages had made men quite familiar with the produce of foreign countries, and the twelfth-century man was not at all a country bumpkin. From Jocelin's *Chronicle* we learn that the Abbot of Flay arrived, and "through his preaching caused the open buying and selling which took place in the market on Sundays to be done away with, and it was ordained that the market should be held on the Monday". Again, as touching on a man's duties and the business practice of the day, we hear that Hamo Bland died without making a will, and this was held to be very discreditable. The horse that was led before the coffin of the deceased was offered to St. Edmund, but the abbot would have nothing to do with it, "for it does not beseem our church to be defiled with the gift of him who died intestate, whom common report accuses of being habitually wont to put out his money to interest. By the face of God, if such a thing come to pass of anyone again in my days, he shall not be buried in the churchyard." Now this must have made it very difficult for the enterprising business men of the twelfth century to get on; yet they did so in quite surprising fashion.

We have referred to the influence of the Crusades in making men familiar with foreign countries; and the practice of going on pilgrimages accustomed them to travelling. In Jocelin's *Chronicle* there is an interesting account of a tremendous walk. Samson had been sent to Rome, in his monk days, by Abbot Hugo, and, returning too late, was put into prison by the abbot, with foot-gyves on him—a sorry return for having braved the dangers of a journey which he thus describes:

> You know what trouble I had for that Church of the Woolpit; how I was dispatched to Rome in the time of the Schism between Pope Alexander and Octavian; and passed through Italy at that Season, when all clergy carrying letters for our Lord Pope Alexander were laid hold of, and some were clapt in prison, some hanged; and some, with nose and lips cut off, were sent forward to our Lord the Pope, for the disgrace and confusion of him. I, however, pretended to be Scotch, and putting on the garb of a Scotchman, and taking the gesture of one, *walked* along; and when anybody mocked at me, I would brandish my staff in the manner of that weapon they call *gaveloc* [like a crowbar], uttering comminatory words after the way of the Scotch.

Samson must needs have been a stout-hearted man to walk to Rome and back, suffer unjust imprisonment and, on emerging from prison, continue to lead a successful life. When he

35   A Twelfth-Century Cart

became abbot we learn he "caused the official person who had, by Abbot Hugo's order, put the fetters on him at his return from Italy, to be supported with food and clothes to the end of his days at Abbot Samson's

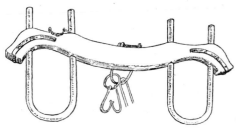

36 An old Sussex Ox-yoke
(*Hastings Museum*)

expense"; but we never hear if he apologised to the Scots for the liberties that he had taken.

And this was not the only long journey Samson made; as a traveller he compared favourably with many modern men. He attended Parliament when the news came that Richard was a prisoner in Germany, and "the abbot started forth in his place in Parliament, and said, that he was ready to go and seek his lord the king, either clandestinely by subterfuge, or by any other method; and search till he found him, and get certain notice of him"; and the abbot went "with rich gifts to the king in Germany". Again, when the monks set out to see the king at Waltham, about the election of a new abbot, they all walked there, their frock-skirts looped over elbow.

Carts(*19, 35*) were not used for travel, and it was considered rather disgraceful to be seen riding in one, probably because the man condemned to death was carted to the gallows. When Launcelot was going to see Queen Guinevere, he lost his horse and, not being able to walk in his armour, he commandeered a cart, with the result that one of the queen's ladies, seeing him from the castle, thought it was a knight "riding to the hanging"; but the queen, recognising Launcelot, reproved her, saying, "it was foul mouthed, and evil compared, so to compare the most noble knight of the world in such a shameful death".

Ladies rode pillion behind a man-servant, or in litters borne between two horses; and nearly all travelling was done on horseback. Only kings and great nobles had special carriages, and the reason of course for this was, that, since the days of the Romans, no good roads had been built: riding was speedier and safer—that is, when they did not walk.

73

Fig. *35* shows a simple farm cart. The oxen drew it by means of the yoke across their shoulders. The yoke was attached to the central pole, which was fastened to the axle. The floor of the cart was framed up on the axle, and the sides made of withes, woven in between upright stakes driven into the edge of the floor. The peasant driving the oxen wears the plain chausses and simple tunic that were the clothing of the working man right through the Middle Ages.

FIELD SPORTS

The Normans were great hunters, and fig. *37* shows a hunting scene. In our chapter dealing with the fifteenth century, a description is given of stag-hunting, taken from a book called *The Master of Game*, written by Edward, Duke of York, who was killed at Agincourt in 1415. As it is supposed that the Normans introduced the method of hunting the stag which is followed to this day, readers are referred to the fifteenth-century chapter (p. 250) for fuller details.

It must have been while hunting, in much the same way as shown, that William Rufus met his death in the New Forest, by an arrow glancing off a tree trunk. It was then, in reality, a new forest, having been enclosed by the Normans to form a game preserve. In the twelfth century the "beasts of the chase" were the buck, doe, and fox; the "beasts of the forest" were the hart and hind; the "beasts and fowls of the warren" were the hare, rabbit, pheasant, and partridge. Henry II's laws

37 Hawking. (*Based on the Bayeux Tapestry*)

forbade anyone to enter a royal forest with bow, arrows, dogs, or greyhounds, save with special warrant, and he forbade the clergy to spend their time in hunting or hawking.

In Jocelin's *Chronicle* we read of Abbot Samson's manor-houses and parks:

> He had laid out several and stocked them with animals, retaining a proper huntsman, with hounds; and, if any guest of great quality were there, our Lord Abbot with his monks would sit in some opening of the woods, and see the dogs run; but he himself never meddled with hunting that I saw.

Now does not that conjure up a pretty picture?

There is another note in Jocelin concerning a quarrel with Richard Cœur-de-Lion. Adam de Cokefield, a feudatory of St. Edmunds, died, leaving a daughter of three months old as his heiress, and she became Abbot Samson's ward, and so could not marry without his consent. Richard wanted to give her in marriage to one of his friends, but the abbot did not approve, and there was a great quarrel; but in the end the abbot had his way—he generally did. "King Richard wrote, soon after, to Abbot Samson, that he wanted one or two of the St. Edmundsbury dogs, which he heard were good"; and, these having been sent, Richard gave the abbot a ring, and so they made it up. No wonder that Abbot Samson appealed to Carlyle as a fine type, worthy of inclusion in "Past and Present".

LAWS AND CUSTOMS

Next we must turn to laws and customs. Before the Conquest the Anglo-Saxons had written laws; and, as the Normans, when they entered England, had none, William's first act was to confirm those already in force which had been made by Edward the Confessor. It must be remembered that William wished to be thought of, not as a conqueror, but as the rightful king of England coming into his own. He protected the Normans, however, by fining the district where one was slain, unless the slayer was produced. Much of the procedure of the old law was traditional, and the laws themselves were only statements of the penalties attaching to wrong-doing. There was very little real development until the time of Henry II. The King's Court was only for the protection of the royal rights, and those of the barons; all other business was conducted at the shire and hundred moots.

Shire moot was held in the open, and presided over by the sheriff; the free landowners had to attend, and they found the dooms, or judgments, but did not try the case. The accused brought forward friends, who swore that he was innocent, and were called oath helpers; or he might be sent to the ordeal of the fire, or the water. He must lift red-hot iron, carry it three paces; his hand was bound up and examined at the end of three days; if blistered he was guilty. Or he was thrown into water, and if he floated was guilty. One is apt to say now: "How absurd!" but that is because of the difficulty we find in understanding the ideas of twelfth-century man. A little boy of our acquaintance gave what is probably the explanation, when he said: "Yes, it would be all right if you really believed it." In the twelfth century it was an old, old custom, and the guilty man, who was perhaps quite ready to swear falsely, would hesitate to undergo the ordeal, and so give himself away, and find the doom given against him.

The Normans introduced the judicial combat, and the combatants fought to show they were right, or else hired somebody else to do it. The weapons used were like pick-axes, made of horn, bound on to wooden handles, the shape of which had come down from bygone ages; they fought, perhaps all day, until the guilty man cried "Craven", when he was promptly hanged. Here again the idea probably was that the man in the right would fight better, and that the other, burdened by a guilty conscience, would give in first.

Henry II made the King's Court the headquarters of justice, and from it the Justices made journeys all over England, and went on circuit just as they still continue to do. But the most important development of Henry II's time was that the sheriff would

38   A Judicial Combat

call in twelve men to give evidence, and so we get the beginnings of our present trial by jury.

Jocelin of Brakelond gives an interesting account of a trial by battle between Henry of Essex and his kinsman, Robert of Montfort, who had accused him of treason and cowardice. Henry was vanquished, and left for dead on the field of battle, but recovered afterwards and turned monk. Another story had a tragic ending: a free tenant of the cellarer, Ketel by name, was charged with theft, and, being the loser in the trial by battle, was hanged. And then follows a most interesting statement, showing how this method of trial was passing. Jocelin reports the burgesses of Bury St. Edmunds as saying: "If that man had only dwelt within the borough, it would not have come to the ordeal, but that he would have acquitted himself by the oaths of his neighbours." The abbot and convent, seeing the truth of this, took steps to remedy this hardship suffered by their tenants.

Samson, as Lord Abbot, had to hold his Court; and on one occasion he had two knights of Risby before him, Willelm and Norman, adjudged to pay the heavy fine of 20s., and this is how he addressed them, in words that throw an interesting side-light on travelling and hospitality:

> "When I was a cloister monk, I was once sent to Durham on business of our Church: and coming home again, the dark night caught me at Risby (where the knights lived), and I had to beg a lodging there. I went to Dominus Norman's and he gave me a flat refusal. Going then to Dominus Willelm's, and begging hospitality, I was by him honourably received. The 20s. therefore of money, I, without mercy, will exact from Dominus Norman; the Dominus Willelm, on the other hand, I, with thanks, will wholly remit the said sum."

"My curse on that Abbot's Court," said another suitor, "where neither gold nor silver can help me to confound my enemy." Truly, the more we hear of Abbot Samson the better we like him.

MEDICINE AND THE CARE OF THE SICK

Twelfth-century medicine and medical treatment were still a curious mixture of quackery and genuine knowledge. Nevertheless, a great school of learning had come into being in the eleventh and twelfth centuries at Salerno in Italy. The legend is that the school was founded by a Jew, a Greek, an

Italian, and a Moor; but the reality underlying the legend is contained in the fact that the study of medicine had its root in these four cultures. On a Greek vase of 400 B.C. we see a representation of a doctor attending his patients. The Greek school of medicine was famous; and Rome carried on the tradition, adding her practical weight in the form of the first hospital system; and Latin treatises on medicine, derived from the Arabic medicinal lore of the Moors in Spain, and usually translated by Jews, were written in the first half of the eleventh century. These treatises contained the nucleus of all medieval medicine. The founding of many European universities in the thirteenth century gave still further impetus to the study, and a school of surgery was started at Bologna.

In the twelfth century, an abbess, near Bingen in Germany, wrote a manuscript on the healing powers of plants, animals, and minerals, with a small additional treatise on the methods of employing medicine.

The monasteries took their share in the care of the sick. Their régime was generally that of kindness, comparative cleanliness, and good food, together with a few simple herbal remedies grown in the monastery garden. The following is an extract from a tenth-century manuscript on drugs:

> For headache take a vessel full of leaves of green rue, and a spoonful of mustard seed, rub together, add the white of an egg, a spoonful, that the salve may be thick. Smear with a feather on the side that is not sore.

Still, even this simple treatment was a great factor in relieving the sufferings of the sick poor, and monastic hospitals or infirmaries existed all over England.

The word hospital has an interesting origin. Guest-houses, "hospitalia", were established in the early Christian era for pilgrims or "hospites" when on pilgrimage. These buildings began also to be used as a refuge for the sick only. The hospital of St. Gregory was founded by Archbishop Lanfranc in 1084, that of St. Bartholomew in 1137, the Holy Cross at Winchester in 1132, and St. Thomas's hospital in 1215.

The growth of any kind of hygiene was very gradual; and in the twelfth and thirteenth centuries dirt, and the lack of any kind of drainage water, rendered all towns noisome places, and encouraged the spread of disease. It was not until after the Black Death in 1348 that the authorities began to recognise the need for some kind of social reform in the care of their cities. It was after this period, and during the Great Plague that swept across Europe in 1374, that the word "quarantine" came into use. Certain Italian cities established a period of isolation for all persons wishing to leave an infected city or to enter an uncontaminated one. The length of time was forty days or "quarantina".

An excellent idea of medical and surgical practice can be obtained from a careful study of two important and attractive medical MSS.—one at Trinity College, Cambridge, of the end of the twelfth or beginning of the thirteenth century, known as O.1.20 (*30–3*). Several drawings show that the doctor was also a druggist, who kept a large stock of herbs, which he weighed out while young assistants pounded and mixed them into potions. It also illustrates the treatment of cataract, trepanning the skull, dealing with ear disease, sewing a neck wound, and extracting an arrow. A case of impetigo, a disagreeable skin rash, is correctly described and graphically illustrated. The text incorporates part of the *Chirurgia* of Roger of Salerno. This should be compared with another MS. of equal human and historic interest in the British Museum, MS. Sloane 1077, just a century later, which, among a number of careful drawings, shows treatment to reduce shoulder dislocation and a type of leg splint—the Gooch—which was re-invented about the middle of the nineteenth century.

We shall see that, later on, drugs were prepared and dispensed at separate pharmacies (p. 189).

Surgery during the early medieval period was regarded as separate from medicine; operations were performed by barbers, bath-keepers, and travelling quacks; and, as late as the time of Frederick the Great, the army surgeon's position was such that he

39 A Physician

was still expected to shave the officers of the regiment. In the twelfth and thirteenth centuries, it was also a dangerous calling, for, should a surgeon operating on his feudal lord fail, he must look forward at least to execution. Yet there were certain great surgeons attached to various Courts throughout the Middle Ages; and the earliest-known English surgeon was John of Arderne, who gained much of his knowledge during the Hundred Years' War. John of Gaddesden, physician to Edward II of England, wrote on medicine, but his work contains many charms and much superstition as well as medical knowledge.

Another celebrated surgeon was Richard of Wendover, who in 1252 wrote an anatomical treatise that still exists. In 1368 a gild was formed by the master surgeons of London. This gild shortly afterwards combined with the physicians, and even recognised women practitioners. They received a royal charter; and barber's surgery was restricted to blood-letting and the healing of wounds. Roger Bacon, a great physician and writer of the thirteenth century, combined with his calling astronomy, mathematics, chemistry or alchemy, and astrology; and indeed all medieval physicians added to their scientific knowledge a profound belief in the additional value of charms and astrology. We are told that Roger Bacon proposed the use of a segment of a glass globe for the benefit of those with aged or defective eyes. The glassworkers of Venice made spectacles in the late thirteenth century; and by the fifteenth century they were in common use among those who could afford them. An expensive luxury, and clumsy in shape, with thick convex lenses, they can be seen in fifteenth-century paintings.

Although anaesthesia was unknown in the Middle Ages, substitutes have always been used throughout the course of history. Surgical sleeping-draughts are frequently mentioned, and one early mixture consisted of hemlock, opium, mulberry juice, hyoscyamus, ivy, mandragora, and lettuce, dried on a sponge. When moistened, it was inhaled by the patient, who was afterwards roused by fennel juice applied to the nostrils.

GAMES AND PASTIMES

Thus we get some idea as to how Norman life was carried on; but we must remember that the Normans played quite as vigorously as they worked. In their spare time they amused themselves with many games of skill and hazard. We read of chess and draughts, both of which seem to have been very popular. The chessmen were carved,

40   Bear-Baiting.
(*From the Bayeux Tapestry*)

generally in whalebone or ivory. An old chronicler, describing various amusements, speaks of chess as the hobby of the wise and of draughts as that of knights, while "the young bachelors pass their time with sham fights and other exercises, also in cock-fighting, bear- or bull-baiting, wrestling, and other sports".

The games of children were miniature copies of those of their elders. Dolls have held their place from time immemorial in the affections of little girls; and boys found the same joy then as they do now in soldiers, spinning-tops, toy horses, whips, and wooden models of many and various kinds. The two boys in fig. *41* are playing with jointed wooden soldiers, which are dressed in the armour of the period. The feet of these figures were weighted with lead to keep the balance, and were jerked backwards and forwards by means of a cord passed through their middle, each boy holding one end of the cord. The arms were jointed as well as the legs, and moved with the motion of the figures; and, with the tightening and slackening of the cord, the little soldiers strutted and pranced, and doubtless waved their arms and swords in a very warlike manner.

41   A game with soldiers

DECORATION

We are giving an illustration or so of illuminated manuscripts for each century, since illumination was one of the most characteristic medieval arts and, besides being extremely beautiful in themselves, the manuscripts reveal much of the spirit and feeling of contemporary life. If you can teach yourself to enjoy these plates (*twelfth century, 34, 70; thirteenth century, 88; fourteenth century, 126-9, 140; fifteenth century, 151, 152, 164-7*), you get to know something of the costume and ornament of each period, and by further study can go on to trace the development in painting and lettering. The manuscripts and their illuminations are of course closely allied to the wall-paintings, stained glass, and carved ornaments of the period. Fig. *70* shows a page from a missal written for Lesnes Abbey, Erith, Kent, about 1200. It has the notes for singing; and the row of pike form the tail of the initial P with its picture of the sacrifice of Isaac at the top.

The tailpiece of this chapter(*42*) illustrates ornament of the period, and helps to explain why the Norman style is sometimes called Romanesque; for here, in this simple design, we can see a survival of a more elaborate Roman pattern. The design might have been used for stone carving, embroidery, or the border to an illuminated manuscript.

Now for a word of advice on design. When drawing pattern, never start putting in the detail until you have got the general line, or structure, complete. In this scroll the main line of the pattern is a wavy one, consisting of more or less half-circles reversed and joined together. From this central line grow other shorter lines, and, unless you get the swing of these "bones" of the pattern, any fine drawing put into the detail will be quite wasted.

This suggests to us that there is no more fruitful study for the designer than real bones. We remember a vertebra of an aurochs we saw in the Gallery of Fossil Mammals in the Natural History Museum at South Kensington. The upward prolongation to assist in carrying the hump made it especially interesting. The lines of the vertebra ran in beautiful curves which flowed into one another in the softest way, and the jointing was wonderful. It should be a source of satisfaction that each of us possesses such an exquisite mechanism. There is a

DECORATION

quip that "if beauty is only skin deep, then ugliness goes to the bone"—it does. If the bones are bad, you cannot have beauty. In architecture the plan of the building is the skeleton. We commend a study of bones, in all their aspects, to any boy or girl who wishes to become a creative artist.

42　Twelfth-Century Ornament

Dates.	Kings and Queens of England and France.	Famous Men.	Great Events, Sea Fights, and Land Battles.	Principal Buildings (B., Benedictine ; C., Cistercian).
1200	John—*Philip Augustus*			Ely Galilee, 1198–1215 Peterborough, west front, B., 1201–14
1203	. . . .	. . . .	Death of Arthur	
1204			Loss of Normandy	Beaulieu Abbey, Hants, C., and St. Mary Overie, Southwark, 1204–38
1207		Stephen Langton, Archbishop		Wells Transepts and Nave, 1206
1212			John excommunicated	
1214	. . . .		Battle of Bouvines	
1215			Magna Charta and Civil War	
1216	Henry III., *m.* Eleanor of Provence	William Pembroke, Earl Marshal		
1217	. . . .	. . . .	Sea fight off Sandwich, and Fair of Lincoln	Wells, west front, 1218–39.
1219		Hubert de Burgh		
1220	. . . .	. . . .	. . . .	Beverly Choir, 1220–25, and Salisbury, 1220–66
1221			Dominicans (Black Friars) come to England	Lincoln Chapter - House, 1220–35
1223	*Louis VIII.*			
1224	. . . .	. . . .	Franciscans (Grey Friars) come to England	
1226	*Louis IX.*			
1228	. . . .	. . . .	Frederick II. crowned King of Jerusalem	
1230	. . . .	. . . .	Crusade of Teutonic Knights against Prussia	
1235	. . . .		. . . .	Ely Presbytery, 1235–51
1236		Matthew Paris becomes historiographer at St. Albans ; *b.* 1200, *d.* 1259		
1242	. . . .	. . . .	Expedition to and loss of Poitou	
1243		Roger Bacon, 1214–1292		
1244		. . . .	Loss of Jerusalem, which remains in Mohammedan hands until 1917	
1245	. . . .	. . . .	. . . .	Westminster Abbey, B, 1245–69, excepting completion of Nave
1248		. . . .	Crusade of St. Louis, 1248–54	
1257		Simon de Montfort	National Rising, 1257–65	
1264	. . . .	. . . .	Battle of Lewes	Beginning Collegiate System, foundation of Merton College, Oxford
1265		Birth of Dante	Battle of Evesham and Simon's Parliament, 1265	
1270	*Philip III.*	. . . .	Crusade of Edward and St. Louis	
1272	Edward I., *m.* Eleanor of Castile			
1274	. . . .	. . . .	Conquest of Wales, 1274-82	
1275	. . . .	. . . .	First Statute of Westminster	
1279			Statute of Mortmain	
1280	. . . .		. . . .	Chester Choir, B., 1280–1315
1282		Llewelyn		
1284	. . . .	. . . .	. . . .	Foundation of Peterhouse College, Cambridge
1285	*Philip IV.*	. . . .	Statute of Winchester	
1289			Death of Queen Eleanor	
1290	. . . .	. . . .	Quia Emptores	St. Etheldreda, Ely Place, Holborn, and York Nave and Chapter-House
1291	. . . .	. . . .	Fall of Acre	Stokesay Castle, Shrops, 1291
1294		William Wallace	Attempted conquest of Scotland and Scotland's alliance with France, which lasts till 1494	
1295			Model Parliament	
1298			Battle of Falkirk	

43   Chart of the "Early English" Period of Design, from 1200 to 1299

44   A Baker of Short-weight Loaves being drawn to the Pillory

Chapter II

THIRTEENTH CENTURY

As we go through the centuries, we shall find that each one
seems to have a character of its own, and that the thoughts
and feelings of the people are reflected in the things that
they have left behind them. In the twelfth century, with which
we dealt in the last chapter, the general impression is that of
rugged strength. The Normans were like their own castles; and
even their cathedrals, beautiful as they are, echo the same
feeling.

In the thirteenth century, England was certainly quieter
and less disturbed; and conditions became far more settled
under the strong reign of Edward I. In 1215 John was forced
to sign Magna Charta, which secured definite rights to every
Englishman. One of its provisions was that "no freeman,
merchant or villein shall be excessively fined for a small offence;
the first shall not be derived of his means of livelihood,
the second of his merchandise, the third of his implements of
husbandry". Meanwhile Parliament showed that it was increasingly able to assert itself. There was also a protracted
struggle between the Church and State for power. The thirteenth
century saw the rise of some great English churchmen, remarkable for their zeal and holiness, such as St. Hugh, Bishop of
Lincoln, and Bishop Grosseteste.

In architecture, the massive solidity of the Norman Romanesque gave place to the lightness and grace of the Early

English style, which we can see in such buildings as Lincoln and Wells cathedrals and Westminster Abbey. Between the massive solidity of the Norman Romanesque building and the lightness and grace of the Early English style, there was a very interesting transition phase in which features of the two styles are combined. Thus, in an arcade, Norman capitals may be surmounted by pointed arches, or capitals with carved leaf foliage may be found under round arches. The greatest examples of the Transitional style are to be admired in some of the Cistercian buildings erected in Yorkshire, among which we may mention the naves of Fountains and Kirkstall. Buildwas is another example; and it is one of the tragedies of architectural history that, owing to their remoteness from towns and villages, these great churches could not be adapted for parish use and have fallen into decay, though they are still beautiful in their ruin. There are a number of Transitional parish churches in the Nene Valley of Northamptonshire, such as Polebrook, Helpstone, and Warmington, and they form a very interesting study.

As we examine the everyday things of the period, we should like our readers to bear in mind that we must think of Westminster Abbey, not as a building put up by Henry III, who though he was a bad king was a good builder, but rather as being symbolical of the aims of a whole people progressing steadily towards a more spacious life—with many setbacks, yet moving forward.

TOWNS AND THE DEVELOPMENT OF TRADE

Towns were growing rapidly. They had first come into being as places of refuge, where communities of people banded together for safety, enclosing their dwellings with a wall. Those who grew surplus produce in the fields outside soon found a ready sale for their goods among citizens who could not till the soil, and the boroughs or towns speedily became centres for every kind of trade and barter.

No community can live without some form of government, and these fast-growing towns were no exception. Councils were set up by the principal citizens, with one man, the mayor, as head, which dealt with all matters concerning the public welfare.

At the same time, from the churches' congregation, societies were formed for social purposes, that members might help each

86

45 "Early English" Costume. Thirteenth Century

other in the hour of need. These societies or gilds, as they were called, were gradually taken over by separate trades; and members of a gild were allowed various privileges, one of which was the right to buy and sell in the town without paying toll. Toll was usually exacted on all goods taken out of one town or brought into another. These gilds not only gave their members privileges, but they exacted also a certain standard of work. Goods were stamped to show that they came up to standard. The hall-mark on modern silver is the mark of a great city company descended from one of those gilds of which we speak.

Banded together in gilds, craftsmen and merchants grew powerful; and, to maintain their rights, the journeymen—that is to say, the men employed by the day (*journée*)—also started gilds for themselves. These men worked independently, and it was not until the sixteenth century that workmen were gathered together by their employer under one roof. This was the beginning of the factory system.

At the end of the fourteenth century emerged the English custom of granting titles to merchants of renown. Michael de la Pole, son of a merchant in Hull, was created Earl of Suffolk. The de la Poles were a great family who played their part in English statecraft, and had a long, chequered and often tragic history, which is part of the troublous times of the latter Middle Ages. You can see their tombs in the fine late Decorated collegiate church of Wingfield in Suffolk, which Michael's father-in-law (Sir John de Wingfield) rebuilt. They had a palace at Ewelme on the Chiltern foothills in Oxfordshire, where William, the first Duke of Suffolk, and his wife Alice built a school and founded almshouses which still survive in delightful red brick. Duchess Alice's tomb in Ewelme church is a lovely piece of craftsmanship, and her effigy lies there in calm serenity, with little angels to smooth her pillow.

COSTUME

We can now turn to the everyday things of the Early English period; and fig. *45* shows what thirteenth-century people looked like. The costume of the period was as simple and beautiful as its architecture. Later on, both became rather overloaded with ornament; but, before this happened, we find in costume the same fitness for purpose and beauty of line as we have already noticed in the architecture of the century. All the garments illustrated are evidently designed for useful wear, and their simple lines are very graceful. Good effects were obtained by the use of fine material, rather than by adding embroidery and jewels.

In this century we find two new garments worn by the richer people: the surcoat, or over-tunic, and the peliçon, or pelisse. The latter, being for outdoor use, was often worn under a cloak in the winter.

In our picture, the lady on the left hand is wearing a cotte, or dress of the period, the skirt of which is not so full as in the twelfth century, and hangs in heavy folds from the waist, which is encircled by a low belt. The sleeves are tight below the elbow, and buttoned to the wrist. The stuffs used for dresses were very beautiful—heavier than those of the twelfth century, and brocaded with gold and silver threads, woven with the design of the fabric, not added afterwards as embroidery. The dress is covered by a fur-lined cloak. The head-dress consists of a fold of linen, or wimple, tied on the top of the head, which was covered by a stiffened cap of the same material.

The second figure is that of a noble; and nobles, with doctors and lawyers, wore their cotte to the ankle; those of the merchants and middle-class men reached to the calf, and the peasants wore theirs to the knee. Over his cotte the nobleman wears a surcoat, with capuchon attached; this surcoat is lined with fur, and has long wide sleeves. His shoes are slightly pointed, and are buttoned round the ankle.

The hair, in this period, was cut in a fringe across the forehead, and at the sides and back of the head reached just below the ears and was curled.

The third figure is a scholar, whose under-garment again is a cotte. Over this he wears a garde-corps, which is really a surcoat of a slightly different shape. This is made of woollen material and lined with fur, and is a rather amusing garment, the arms coming through a slit in front of the hanging sleeves, and the fastening in front going part-way down and coming part-way up.

The head-dress is a small cap or coife, over which was drawn the capuchon. The capuchon, or chaperon, was the chief medieval head-dress, which, starting from quite early times, lasted until the days of the Tudors. In shape like a long sugar-loaf,

90

it had a hole for the face in one of its sides, the lower half being pulled down over the shoulders as a cape, and the upper half hanging down at the back as a liripipe.

The fourth figure is a little girl clad in a cotte of some light material, and over it she wears a bliaut, a tunic only worn indoors, fitting closely to the figure at the top, springing out at the waist, cut wide and long in the skirt, and without sleeves. Since she is a child, she wears her hair loose on her shoulders, with a plain circlet around the head. The doll follows the same style as her mistress.

The nurse with the little girl is wearing a pelisse, and the capuchon attached is drawn over her head. The pelisse was an outdoor garment, very much like the garde-corps, but fuller and longer; under this the figure is shown wearing the usual cotte, and a wimple on the head like the first lady.

The peasant wears a plain tunic with a capuchon, has plain cloth chausses on his legs, and shoes of heavy felt or cloth, or sometimes leather. On these, in wet weather, he would wear clogs of wood, such as are worn by the man weeding in the illustration that depicts fourteenth-century agriculture(*120*).

46   Thirteenth-Century Ecclesiastic Costume

In the illustrations(*46, 47*) the costumes of the Monastic and Military Orders are shown. The figure on the left-hand side of fig. *46* is a Crusader; he wears banded mail with a white surcoat, with a red cross on his breast. The helm is an interesting thirteenth-century development. It was found that the nose-piece, or nasal, shown in fig. *1* on the Norman knight, was rather dangerous in use, because the enemy could take hold of it; and, when so held, the knight was at his opponent's mercy. To prevent this, the nasal was lengthened, and the whole face covered in with the exception of eye-slits. The top of the helm was made flatter than in Norman times, and the effect must have been very much that of a saucepan without its handle.

The second and third figures in fig. *46* are a Benedictine monk and nun; both wear long black robes—that of the monk has a cowl which can be drawn over the head, and the nun wears a white wimple under her black hood.

The left-hand figure in fig. *47* is a pilgrim. He is shown wearing the ordinary dress of the period, to which are added the signs of his pilgrimage—the wide hat and rough cloak, which sometimes had a cross on the shoulder, signifying that

he had made a pilgrimage to Palestine. He carries a staff with a hook on it to take his bundle, and a scrip, or purse. These were always blessed by his priest when he started. His beard and hair were allowed to grow. When a pilgrim returned from the Holy Land, he was entitled to wear a piece of palm in his hat: hence he was sometimes called a palmer. Those who had been to Rome wore lead

47   Thirteenth-Century Ecclesiastic
Costume

or pewter signs which they obtained there, bearing the effigies of St. Peter, St. Paul, or the crossed keys. Those of the Compostella pilgrimage bore scallop shells on their hat, the sign of St. James. From Canterbury they brought away an ampul, or flask, containing a few drops of the blood of St. Thomas à Becket, and they also carried bells.

The right-hand figure is a Knight Templar. He is shown wearing a hauberk, and chausses of banded mail, an interesting development of that shown in fig. *1*. The banded mail was formed by rows of flat rings slightly overlapping and sewn on to leather, stout linen, or coloured velvets. One row of rings was laid one way, and the next the other way; and the material on to which they were sewn was gathered into a little tuck, enclosing a cord, which separated the rows and kept the rings flat, and gave a stronger finish than the earlier method. The Templar wears a white surcoat over his hauberk. This is supposed to have been introduced by the Crusaders because the sun of the East made their coat of mail unbearably hot. Though first adopted for a very practical purpose, the surcoat developed into beautiful jupons or tabards, emblazoned at a later period with the armorial bearings of the knight.

All Knights Templars wore a white cloak with a red cross on the shoulder, a red cap, with white undercap, and carried a staff

48   Armourers at Work

with a shield on top ornamented with a red cross on a white ground. The staff was of metal, and often used as a weapon. Their beard and hair were worn long.

Even the horses were given a coat of mail(*48*). The armourer's craft from now on became a very important one.

SHIPS AND SEA-FIGHTS

Drawings of Crusaders and Templars remind us of the Holy Land; so our illustration(*49*) shows the ships in which they sailed there.

This is interesting, since it explains why we still talk of fore-castle—in the thirteenth century a ship really did have fore and stern castles. The Crusades exercised a great influence on our ships, as they did on all the arts and crafts. When they took their viking-like ships into the Mediterranean, the Crusaders were greatly impressed by the developments they noticed in Eastern shipping. There is an illuminating account of a Saracen ship, attacked by the fleet of Richard Cœur-de-Lion, near Beirut, in Syria, in 1191. This ship is said to have had three masts, and carried 1,500 men, which sounds like an exaggeration; but she must have been considerably larger, and better found, than anything they had yet seen. Her tall sides presented a formidable obstacle to Richard's men in their attack from lower boats. The Saracen ship was eventually rammed by galleys, and taken, with her sides stove in. The *White Ship* of Henry I, which went down in 1120, and was probably one of our best boats, is supposed to have had fifty oars, and carried three hundred people. It is shown in old manuscripts as having only one mast.

In these early days, sea fights were rather like land battles, the idea being to get to close quarters; no damage could be done to the enemy outside the range of a bow-shot (about 300 yards), so the fight speedily resolved itself into hand-to-hand conflict. This tall ship of the Saracens must have set our boat designers thinking, because it exposed an assailant to the disadvantage of being *under* the enemy's fire. The first step taken to counteract this disadvantage was the setting up of castles in the bow and stern; and in the earlier types, like the ships shown on the seals of Sandwich, Winchelsea, and Hastings, all of which date from the thirteenth century, the castles

94

49   A Ship of the time of Edward I, based on the Dover seal, 1284

have very little connection with the structure of the boat, and
resemble high raised platforms, which, in fact, is what they
were—perches for the archers, whence they could fire *down* on
to the enemy's decks. This type is shown on the small boat in
the distance.

These detached castles were not very beautiful, and did not
long satisfy the naval architects of the day. In the Dover seal,
which dates from 1284, we see the next development; and it is
this ship that we have drawn.

The hull, or body of the boat, remains much the same as the
Norman ship, and is on the old Viking lines. There is one mast
and a square sail; but a fighting top has been added, where an
archer could be stationed. The fore and stern castles are
developed and, instead of being independent raised platforms,
are now joined up to the structure of the boat, and, just like
castles on the land, have embrasures through which the archers

95

could shoot, with merlons in between to protect them. Under the platform, the supporting posts have very graceful arches between them, similar in detail to the land architecture of the period. The space thus partially enclosed was the beginning of the cabin; there is a sort of elementary bowsprit, and at the end is a bowline comb to take the bowlines which go to the mainsail. There is not any great advance in the rigging, and the steering is still done by means of an oar on the starboard side.

Fig. *50* demonstrates how the trebuchet, which was used for sieges on land(*59*, *60*), was at a very early date mounted on board ship. Our illustration has been made from a drawing in the manuscript of *The Romance of Alexander*, at Trinity College, Cambridge. The narrative is in French verse, by Eustace, or Thomas, of Kent, and the drawings, in the St. Albans style, are in lively outline in red and green ink. The manuscript dates from about 1250. We have added rowers, because there must have been some motive power, and sails would not have been practicable. In all other respects we have followed the original drawing.

50   A Thirteenth-Century Man-of-War

96

There were also great developments in castle-building during the thirteenth century. We saw in fig. *22* how at Orford the architect developed the design of the keep until it became a marvel of ingenuity; from the purely military point of view, on the other hand, it was not so successful. At Orford, after the besiegers had stormed the bailey, and driven the garrison into the keep, all they had to do was to sit down and starve them out. If a head appeared at a window, an arrow soon sent it in again, and the boxed-up garrison had no chance of surprising the attackers by making a sortie.

To trace the next stage in castle-building, we must go to North Wales. Here Edward I had to carry on the work begun by the Conqueror. Being a great soldier, instead of following the Welshmen into the hills, he blocked the passes and, supported by his fleet, built a series of castles in key positions. In conjunction with the castles, royal boroughs were founded— at Caernarvon and Conway in 1284; Criccieth, Harlech, and Bere, 1285; Beaumaris, 1295; Newborough, 1303; Bala, 1324; and Nevin and Pwllheli in 1355. These boroughs were colonised with English settlers attracted by privileges granted to them as burgesses of the boroughs. They became centres of English influence; and Caernarvon, which is the subject of our illustrations(*51, 52*), and was begun in 1285, is one of these boroughs. The wild Welsh who saw the walls rising, as shown in fig. *52*, must have understood that they were "up against it".

Caernarvon commands the entrance to the Menai Strait; and it is situated at the mouth of the river Saint, which afforded anchorage for the ships of war we have shown. The town, or borough, was like a large outer bailey added to the castle, and here the English settlers lived. Even to-day parts of the walls remain.

Turning to fig. *52*, which gives a bird's-eye view of the actual castle, the first thing to note is that Caernarvon differs considerably from Orford. It is not so much a castle as a fortified wall. Not only are these walls topped with the usual battlements (*51*), but there are two galleries beneath contrived in the thickness of the walls. It is obvious that, when the walls were manned, a perfect broadside of arrows could be discharged by

51   The Battlements of Caernarvon

the archers. On the north side of the castle, the arrow slits are ingeniously arranged, so that three archers could shoot out of a single opening. Fig. *51* shows an archer on the battlements. He is firing through an arrow slit pierced in the merlon, or masonry between the ordinary embrasures.

The next point to be noted is that the salient angles of the walls are guarded by projecting towers, so that archers could fire along the faces of the adjoining walls, if besiegers attempted to raise scaling ladders. Each tower formed a place of refuge to which the garrison could retreat, even if their opponents breached the walls and gained an entry into the bailey. Again, the castle does not rely upon a single entrance; it has no less than five; so that the garrison, if hard pressed at one, could make a sortie from another.

This must be remembered; for, if any of our readers pay a visit to Caernarvon, once inside the castle they may well lose sight of the simplicity of the plan in what seems to be a confusion of towers, battlements, and galleries.

The main king's gate at 3(*52*) had a drawbridge outside, with portcullises at either end of the passage. This had "murder holes" in the vault over it, from which boiling liquids could be poured down on attackers who forced the outer door, or portcullis. Alternatively, they could be shot by arrows from the guard-rooms at the side. This gateway led into the outer bailey at 4. Here were the barracks for the garrison and the stables for their horses. The constable of the castle lived in the rooms in the tower over the gate.

The inner bailey was cut off from the outer bailey by a range of buildings. There was a passage-way through, called the black

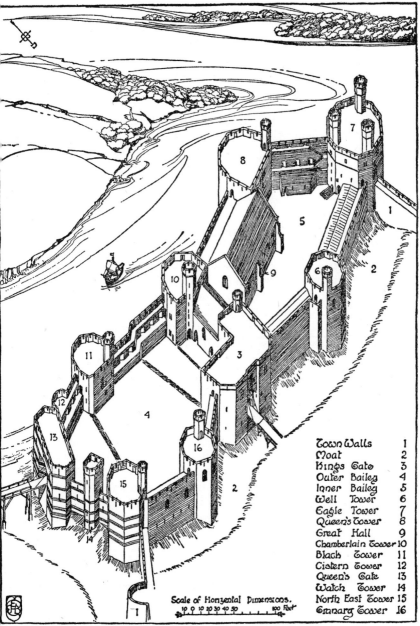

Town Walls 1
Moat 2
Kings Gate 3
Outer Bailey 4
Inner Bailey 5
Well Tower 6
Eagle Tower 7
Queen's Tower 8
Great Hall 9
Chamberlain Tower 10
Black Tower 11
Cistern Tower 12
Queen's Gate 13
Watch Tower 14
North East Tower 15
Granary Tower 16

Scale of Horizontal Dimensions.
10 0 10 20 30 40 50 100 Feet

52   A Bird's-eye View of Caernarvon Castle, North Wales

99

alley, which itself was defended by portcullises at either end. The great hall, in the inner bailey at 9, must have been used as the general living-room. It was certainly the pleasantest place in the castle. The rooms in the towers are gloomy, lighted by the merest slits of windows, recessed in the very thick walls— walls so thick that, in some cases, the galleries in the curtain walls are carried round outside the tower rooms. The kitchens were built against the curtain wall, in the inner bailey, between the king's gate, 3, and the well tower, 6. The well here still contains good water. There was a postern gate from the inner bailey on to a wooden quay, and a water gate from the eagle tower.

The part of the castle that stretches from the eagle tower, 7, to just beyond the chamberlain tower, 10, was built between 1285 and 1291; so that the birth of Edward II, the first Prince of Wales, could not have taken place in the eagle tower on 25 April 1284, as the tradition once was. It may be that he was born in the keep of the old Norman castle, which stood where the outer bailey, 4, now is, and was not removed for some time. The next section continued round to the north-east tower, 15, between 1295 and 1301; and the remaining portion of the north front, necessary to complete the curtain up to the eagle tower, was built between 1315 and 1322. Though building operations went on for some thirty-seven years, Caernarvon gives the impression of having been constructed according to a single plan. The castle gains very considerably in appearance from the bands of Aberpwll stone which enliven the plain limestone of the general wall. As plans go, Caernarvon was better from the military point of view, but not nearly so ingenious or so complete a thing as Orford. It remains a fortified wall, against which, on the inside, were run up sheds and halls and kitchens.

The Liberate Rolls of Henry III, who was a great builder, are full of instructions to the keepers of his various castles and manor-houses. This is how one of them reads:

> The constable of Marlborough Castle is ordered to cleanse the great ditch round Marlborough Castle and to repair it with new bays. And to make a bell-turret on the western end of the chapel of St. Nicholas there, and new lists between the aforesaid chapel of St. Nicholas and the king's kitchen; and a great round window over the king's seat in the great hall there, and to crenellate the

100

wall of the castle between the king's chamber and the great tower. He is to make also a certain great chamber at Ludgershall, for the use of Edward, the king's son, with two chimneys and two privy-chambers; and to remove the old kitchen to beside the new kitchen behind the king's hall there; and to make an image of the Blessed Mary with her Child in the chapel of St. Leonard there.

All this seems to prove that the various halls, kitchens, and other necessary rooms were built against the inside of the curtain walls wherever it was convenient to do so; and, when we are describing the smaller houses of this period, we shall see that they consisted of a group of buildings around the hall, rather than one complete building, all under the same roof.

Just one more point must be made before we leave Caernarvon. Our readers may be sometimes puzzled by finding a castle that appears to have a twelfth-century keep, thirteenth-century outer ward, and fourteenth-century gatehouse. The explanation, of course, is that the castle builders, like the cathedral builders, always built in the spirit of their own age, and did not copy the work which had gone before. So the keep was retained because it was useful, and the remaining defences were remodelled and improved from time to time.

THE CONCENTRIC CASTLE

After Caernarvon we come to Harlech; and this castle, fig. *53*, gives us a chance to indulge in a little practical philosophy. It is extremely probable that some of the boys and girls who read this book will become architects or engineers. They may dream dreams, and see visions of fine buildings or great bridges that span mighty chasms; but unless they can find clients who will back them, then their castles will remain suspended in the air. Now think of the architect who was called in to assist Edward I in his castle-building in North Wales. He was asked to design, not one, but many castles, and as he built them he could try out all his ideas and improve on them as he went along; and the ideas gained in building castles became of use later on when houses were wanted.

If we turn to page 97 we find that foundation charters were granted to Caernarvon and Conway in 1284; so these were the first of the North Wales castles; and in both buildings the plan consists, not of a keep, but a strongly fortified curtain

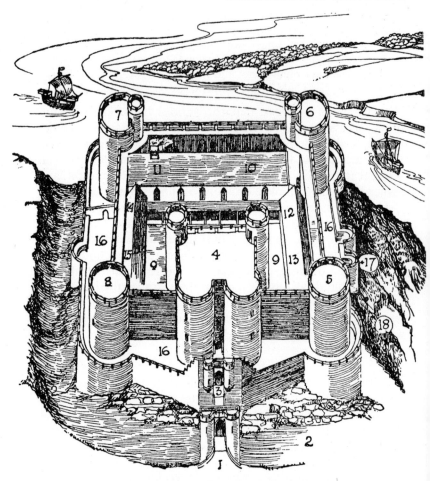

53   A Bird's-eye View of Harlech Castle, North Wales

1	Barbican	7	Bronwen Tower	13	Bakehouse
2	Moat	8	Mortimer Tower	14	Ystumgwern Hall
3	Outer Gate	9	Inner Ward	15	Granary
4	Gatehouse	10	Great Hall	16	Middle Ward
5	Prison Tower	11	Kitchen	17	Postern
6	Armourer's Tower	12	Chapel	18	Outer Ward

wall. Harlech followed in 1285, and it looks as if the architect
said to himself: "Yes, Caernarvon was not so bad, but if one
wall is good, two would be better." So at Harlech there are two
walls, as there are at Beaumaris of 1295. The outer range is
known as the list walls. Hugh Braun, in his fascinating study,

102

The English Castle, explains that it was imperative to keep the
besiegers farther away from the walls, so as to oblige their siege
engines to fire at longer range. We must also remember the
increased effectiveness of the bow. A shaft from a long bow was
no joke; at full force it could pierce plate armour at something
like 200 yards. Mr. Braun's clever little sketch gives a restored
layout of Beaumaris, as do G. T. Clark's earlier drawings.
Beaumaris represents the castle-builders' last word in mighty
defensive strength (*54–6*); later castle buildings became
increasingly residential; while the cannon developed into a
destructive force that no fortress could withstand. This is now
called the concentric type of castle. It was new to England in
the thirteenth century, but was a type that was very old in the
East. Herodotus tells us how the Persians, in 538 B.C., built the
city of Agbatana with seven circular walls, each one higher than
the one outside it.

This was the true concentric principle, and we have endeavoured to fit it into its place in our book on *Ancient Greece.*
It may have reached England through a Crusader. Being
constitutionally very lazy people, we have taken the greatest
pains with fig. *53*, because we hope that it will save lengthy
descriptions of Harlech. The double walls are clearly shown,
with the narrow middle ward between them at 16. Any
besieging force trying to scale the outer wall would have been
under fire from the battlements of the inner wall; and, if they
gained the middle ward, all kinds of missiles could have been
dropped on them. Assuming the attackers did breach the inner
walls, the garrison could retire to the towers and carry on the
fight there. The arrangement of the buildings in the inner ward,
at 9, is less haphazard than at Caernarvon, and more like that
of a house. It closely resembles Bodiam, built in 1386 (*101*).

Harlech stands on a rocky cliff, below which marshes stretch
to the sea; but when it was built there was a harbour here. It is
thought that the river Dwyryd passed under the castle rock (*53*),
and joined the sea somewhat to the south-west of the castle. So
where the harmless golfer now indulges in his innocent game of
striking and seeking little white balls, Edward's ships once sailed
to visit his garrisons.

We hope we have said enough to indicate the military
considerations that influenced the old castle-builders. People

54   The Gateway

55   Bird's-eye View

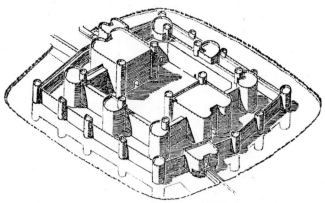

56   Bird's-eye Reconstruction by Hugh Braun, F.S.A.

BEAUMARIS CASTLE, ANGLESEY

sometimes talk about the prettiness of an old castle ruin, as if its builders had purposely designed it as a ruin, to add charm to a bend in a river, or cap the outline of a seaside cliff. But the more we study the plans and remains of old castles, the more struck we are by the great ingenuity shown in their planning, and the remarkable way in which they served their purpose. The history of warfare is full of tales of this constant duel between offence and defence; and the principle is the same, whether we are discussing a castle and its besiegers, the armour of a warship and the gun whose shell can pierce it, or a submarine and its destroyer. To take the middle example, a new and harder steel is invented; and for a while the gun is behind-hand and cannot damage the ship; then it does do so, and the shipbuilder puzzles his wits to go one better.

In the case of the medieval castles, their designers did their work so well that, in the end, before the use of gunpowder, the only way of inducing the defenders to surrender was the very lengthy one of cutting off all supplies and starving them out.

SIEGE-CRAFT AND ENGINES OF WAR

In the next few illustrations (*57–60*) we have tried to show the construction of the chief engines used in medieval siege warfare. To understand the use of these machines, our readers should turn to the pages of Froissart's *Chronicles*. Froissart, of course, lived later, in the time of Edward III, and wrote of the doings of the Black Prince; but he evokes the atmosphere of the Middle Ages as no one else does. It was Sir Walter Scott who said: "Whoever has taken up the chronicle of Froissart must have been dull indeed if he did not find himself transported back to the days of Cressy and Poictiers"; and elsewhere: "We hear the gallant knights arrange the terms of the combat and the manner of the onset; we hear their soldiers cry their war-cries; we see them strike their horses with the spur; and the liveliness of the narration hurries us along with them into the whirlwind of battle." We gain an impression from Froissart's pages of the very slight pretexts on which people went to war, and how intensely they enjoyed it. Yet despite the brutality of medieval warfare, it also had its friendly side, with something of the character of a sporting trial of strength.

Now as to the methods of besieging a thirteenth-century

castle. The first proceeding was to draw two lines of strong palisaded fencing around it; the inner was called the contravallation, and the outer circumvallation. These had their gates; and the space inside, which must have resembled a small town, was used by the besiegers for their tents, to house their siege train, and the stores that would have been necessary. The object of these lines was to prevent surprise by sorties on the part of the garrison, or armed relief from their friends outside, and to prevent any supplies reaching the besieged. All this preparatory work is some explanation of the length of time taken over the old sieges. The defence would be tested in various places and the weakest spot chosen for attack(125). Assuming that the wall on the right hand of the picture had been selected, the moat was filled up by means of a movable shed, called a cat or sow, which was probably used at night. Made of strong timbers, with a steeply sloping roof to throw off stones, and covered with raw hides to resist fire, it had also a little pent roof in front to protect the engineers who, under cover of it, threw down faggots, earth, stones, or anything else that would fill up the moat. Thus they formed a causeway, across which it could be pushed on rough planks laid on top of the bank. Once it had arrived at the walls, the besieged would do their best to set the sow on fire, or to crush it by dropping anything of weight they possessed(125); but on a dark night, with only the light of torches to show the besiegers, their task must have been a difficult one, and they themselves an easy mark for bowmen. Mining operations would be begun, and a hole made in the wall by the use of crowbars; or a battering-ram slung by chains from the roof of the cat, and shod with iron at the end, would be swung backwards and forwards until the same purpose was effected. The engineers' task was made easier by a habit that medieval builders had of only facing their walls with worked stones, and filling in the middle with rough rubble, sometimes very loose and badly cemented together with mortar of poor quality. To combat the activities of the engineers in mining walls, the early castle-builders constructed external wooden galleries on the tops of the curtain walls, so that, through their floors, they could more safely hurl stones and pour down boiling liquids on those working below. It was to smash up these wooden galleries that the medieval military engineers brought into use engines similar to those employed by the Greeks and Romans. In the twenty-sixth chapter of Second Chronicles we read that "Uzziah prepared for them throughout all the host shields, and spears, and helmets, and habergeons, and bows, and slings to cast stones. And he made in Jerusalem engines, invented by cunning men, to be on the towers and upon the bulwarks, to shoot arrows and great stones withal." The Greeks and Romans used catapults that shot darts and arrows, and ballistas for throwing stones. Their propelling force was obtained by the use of twisted skein, prepared, according to a secret method, from various hairs and gut, so that it was very strong and did not lose elasticity. The principle on which this worked can be illustrated by taking a piece of string and tying the two ends together; let one boy then loop a finger into the circle and pull, and another boy do the same, so that the double piece of string is pulled tight between them; then put in the end of a piece of stick, and with it twist the string round and round; let go the stick, and it will fly round in the opposite direction. The engine in fig. *58* is a ballista of this type, sometimes called a mangon. The arm which is pulled down is fixed at the end into a great cable-like coil of tightly twisted skein. The man pulled down the cup-shaped top, and put into it a stone shot weighing perhaps 2 cwt. The arm was released by an ingenious trigger and flew up against the cross-framing at the top of the machine, with the result that the stone was lobbed over the walls, or against the wooden galleries. The trebuchet was the chief

57   An Arblast

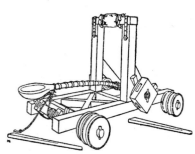

58   A Mangon ready for loading
Reconstructed by Hugh Braun, F.S.A.

59   Loading a Trebuchet

medieval weapon, and was first introduced by the French in the twelfth century; two of these are shown in figs. 59 and 60. This acted on the principle of a counterweight; a long arm was pivoted on a very strong framing, and had suspended from it at one end a large box which would be filled with stones, old iron, or lead. At the other end was a sling, in which was placed a stone shot, and a bridle was attached to the sling from the arm, which ensured that the stone was pitched out at the right moment. The arm was wound down by a windlass, and the sling disposed in the trough at the foot of the framing. The trigger touched off, the counterweight came into action, and off flew the stone to smash through a roof. Sometimes barrels of flaming tar would go over the walls, or dead horses, which gives one an idea of the size of the trebuchets; or they would pitch over filthy refuse to breed a plague, or truss up some unwary sentry whom they had captured, and send him whirling back to a painful death. The trebuchet was also called petrary, onager, scorpion, perrier, and catapult by medieval writers. The machine like a large crossbow was called an arblast or espringale (57) and shot iron javelins. This acted on the same principle as the ballista—by pulling back an arm, which when released hit the javelin and sent it whistling through the air. We have met Shropshire people called Arblaster, which sounds rather terrifying; they are no

60   A Powerful Trebuchet
Reconstructed by Hugh Braun, F.S.A.

doubt descended from an ancestor who, in the Middle Ages, worked an arblast.

It was these machines that necessitated the corbelling forward of the battlements, so that the defenders could pour down stones and shoot at the besiegers mining under, without being so much exposed as they were in the wooden galleries. This feature was called machicolation, and was introduced in the latter part of the thirteenth century.

But we must now return to the engineers mining the walls. They made as large a hole as they could, and inserted wooden props and struts, which were then fired; and, if the work had been well done, some considerable portion of the wall was breached, and the besiegers stormed in over the ruins, and a fierce hand-to-hand fight might give them possession of the outer ward. It was then that the towers became useful; for it was to them that the garrison retreated. These towers were large, each of them in itself as strong as a twelfth-century keep, and access was gained to them only through narrow and easily defended doors. Once possession of the bailey was obtained in a twelfth-century castle, there remained only the keep; but the besiegers of the thirteenth-century castle found that by breaching the curtain wall of the outer ward at one place, they gained possession of that point alone; and with all the towers intact, and arranged to flank the space inside, they were under concentrated bow fire, exposed at any moment to attack, and in reality not much better off.

The beffroi, a movable tower, was another medieval machine used for siege purposes, where mining operations by engineers were not possible. It was worked like the cat, or sow, by filling up the moat in front as it was pushed across the gradually lengthening causeway. Framed up in timber, it was covered with the raw hides of the cattle killed in camp, the hair being placed inside, as a protection against arrows discharged with strands of flaming tow to set the tower on fire. Ladders at the back led to several floors, in which the men-at-arms were crowded against the signal for attack. A drawbridge was lowered when the tower reached the walls, and across this the assailants surged (*125*), and in the fierce *coup de main* many must have fallen into the moat.

Such was the position until gunpowder was introduced; but

61   A Thirteenth-Century Siege

even then the trebuchet held its own for a long time against the early type of cannon. Any reader who enjoys lively accounts of medieval fortress sieges should consult *Annals of a Fortress* by the great French architect Viollet-le-Duc, translated by Bucknall. In it he takes an imaginery fortified town and gives vivid descriptions of the sieges it underwent from Roman times to the Napoleonic wars.

THE MEDIEVAL HALL

Our drawing(62) is of a hall, such as the one built in the inner bailey at Caernarvon; but, before we describe its details, we must thoroughly understand the uses to which it was put. In our twelfth-century chapter we drew attention to the fact that the hall, surrounded by its bowers, was the Anglo-Saxon type of house, and that this design continued to exist side by side with the Norman castles, and was developed by the monks, when building their manor-houses, into a more comfortable form of dwelling. In the thirteenth century the hall was further developed, and we find that it was the keypoint, or centre, of almost every kind of building. In the monastery the refectory was the hall; in the colleges which were founded at Oxford and Cambridge during this century, the hall was the place of general assembly where the students were fed and taught, and their lodgings were grouped around it. The old college buildings still remaining to-day give the best idea of a medieval building. The Manor House of a country village is still often called the Hall, and this is another indication of the importance that used to be attached to this part of the house. In it people lived, had their meals, played games—and in those days grown-up people romped; the young men could fence, or have some cudgel play; the dogs came in and joined in the fun, found bones thrown on to the floor, and fought; and at night the servants slept there in the rushes or on rough beds. So, if we want to understand the Middle Ages, we must not think of the hall as a gloomy, linoleumed square with the front door at one end and the stairs at the other. The medieval hall was a very different, and much more spacious and hospitable place.

In shape the hall was oblong, having the high table at one end, where the lord and his family dined; the other tables shown in the illustration were just plain boards clamped together, and

111

62   A Thirteenth-Century Hall ("Early English" style)

laid on trestles rather like a carpenter's sawing-stool, so that they could be cleared away, leaving a large, open space. The chair on the left shows that the better type of furniture was of a design that we associate nowadays with churches. Then there would be benches like school forms; chests in which arms and

112

63   A Laver

general oddments could be put away, and what were called livery cupboards. One of these is shown beyond the chair, and would be for the use of the servants, who kept their belongings here, and the salts. The piece of furniture used by the family for the same purpose was called a court cupboard.

An inventory of the furniture of a hall in 1311 is given as 2 pots, 3 lavers, boards and trestles (*108*) and other necessaries; and in 1397 we are told there were 2 dorsars, 2 bankers, 2 pieces of ware, 2 brass lavers, 2 large pots, 1 bowl of brass, 2 andirons and 1 poker of iron, 3 boards with trestles and one fixed, 2 chairs, 3 benches and 3 stools.

The dorsars spoken of in the inventory were pieces of tapestry which hung over the backs of the chairs; and the bankers were cushions or sometimes only pieces of embroidered cloth placed on the seats of the chairs or benches.

Lavers (*63*) were for the use of guests before and after meals. Small basins of metal for the washing of hands, they were handed to visitors at the high table by pages who also held napkins for drying. Lesser guests and retainers could use fixed basins at the entrance to the hall. When we remember that there were no forks, and that fingers usually took their place, it is obvious that the laver was a very necessary piece of equipment.

The dais at the end of the hall on which stood the high table, used by the master of the house and his guests, was usually overhung by a canopy of embroidered silk or woolcloth; and we must not forget that except for the master's solar or private apartment, which was both his sleeping- and sitting-room, the hall was the only room in the house. Separate buildings, generally of wood, were added on as required, connected when necessary with passages also of wood.

In the Liberate Rolls of Henry III we read of a passage thus erected "that the Queen might walk from her chamber to chapel with a dry foot".

At Woolmer, the castle of Edward I was built entirely of wood, the interior decorated with painted plaster and roofed with wood shingles.

64   Bellows

During the Coronation ceremonies of Edward I in 1273, all the ground within the palace enclosure was covered with wooden buildings of various kinds—lodgings for guests, halls for their meals and recreations, and kitchens. These kitchens were no more than sheds, and huge fires were lighted outside, over which were hung the cauldrons for boiling various meats and other food. The confusion outside the palace, within the precincts, must have been amazing—cooks, scullions and hangers-on, beggars, men-at-arms, pages, all hurrying about their various businesses: piles of faggots and chopped wood for the fires: provisions, meats, tubs of water: stables with forges and farriers: in fact, a more or less self-supporting community would have been accommodated there. Such a scene, with no water except such as could be carried by hand, no drainage of any kind and no light save that of torches or candles, is almost impossible for the modern mind to picture.

Other attachments to a large house or castle were the sewery, which contained the table furnishings and household linen, and the wardrobe, where stuffs that had been purchased were stored until they were needed, together with extra hangings and robes.

65   Bakers

All valuables, cups, ewers and basins of precious metals, spices, gold, Eastern sugars, as well as candlesticks and plates, were kept in the wardrobe, and in the buttery were stored wines and beer, the latter being generally brewed at home. Henry III had mattresses in his household

114

covered with silk and velvet, besides pillows and bolsters, linen sheets, and fine counterpanes and rugs made of wool.

The same king, too, as we shall see (p. 132), was fond of gardens, and we hear of cherry-trees being ordered for the gardens of Westminster, and of the purchase of vines, roses, willows, and mulberry-trees.

The fireplace is shown against the wall, but it was more often placed in the middle of the floor, as shown in our illustration of a fourteenth-century hall(*105*), and continued to occupy this position until Elizabeth's time.

The windows are typical of the Early English period of design, the tracery being made up of circles and plain geometrical patterns. Glass was beginning to appear in the royal palaces, but had hardly come into common use. The walls were plastered, not quite so mechanically as nowadays, but with a thinner coat, which did not altogether conceal the stone beneath, and produced a much softer and more agreeable effect than the dead smooth surface of the modern room. On this were painted diaper patterns like the one shown, or figures of the saints with golden stars; and wooden wainscoting was often added.

Meanwhile, the colours of dresses were becoming brighter: joyous colours were typical of the Middle Ages. The costumes of the period have already been illustrated; and both the houses in which these people lived and the churches in which they worshipped were splashed about with the three primary colours of red, blue, and yellow, with a little gold thrown in. Perhaps this love of colour accounts for the merriness of Old England: it is difficult to be dull if you are garbed like a cheerful parrot.

Now as to the roof. In the twelfth-century hall it will be remembered that a very beautiful stone arch helped the old builders to overcome the difficulty of bridging across a wide space; and, as this hall was nearly square in shape, one arch across the middle divided it into two narrower oblongs, which could easily be spanned by timbers. But the shape of the thirteenth-century hall was oblong, and many arches would have been necessary. So the principal was invented—the name given to the series of strutted beams that cross the hall down its length. The large beams themselves are called tie-beams, since they help to tie in the walls; they rest on timbers running along the tops of the walls, called wall-plates. Into the undersides of the tie-beams are tenoned wall-posts which rest on stone corbels, and between the wall-post and tie-beam is a curved strut, or brace, which serves the purpose of picking up some of the weight of the roof and transferring it to the wall some way down. At the centre of each tie-beam is a short post, which later on is to develop into the king-post. This supports the ridge which runs across from principal to principal; and the other large timbers performing the same function are called purlins. The smaller timbers resting on top of the purlins, and going the same way as the tie-beams, are called rafters. These are crossed by the roof-boarding, and on the roof-boards would be laid the final lead covering. So here we have the beginning of the timber-framed roofs that in the succeeding centuries add so much to the beauties of church and hall.

CHURCH-BUILDING

Our illustration(66) is of a thirteenth-century or Early English vaulted roof to the aisle of a church—the aisle being selected as showing the principle of the construction in a simpler way than is possible with the usually more elaborate and larger vaults of the nave or choir. In the twelfth century, we saw how the Normans developed the plain barrel vault, which was said to be like an ordinary railway tunnel, by crossing it with other vaults of the same shape. In this thirteenth-century roof we get much the same sort of thing; only, instead of a semicircular railway tunnel crossed by others of the same shape, we now have a pointed one. The groins, or diagonal ribs crossing each bay of the vault from angle to angle, are semicircular in true elevation (67, 3). If the reader turns back to the description of the Norman vaulting, this will perhaps be made clearer. The arches across the aisle have now disappeared, and their place is taken by moulded stone ribs. These are much the same as the diagonals, or groins, and those against the walls; but there is not as yet one at the top or ridge of the vault.

These ribs were probably introduced, not only because they improved the general appearance of the vault, but because their employment saved the use of wood. The Norman vaults were more or less cast, like plum-puddings, on boards, laid on what are called centres of the shape of the vault; and this must have

66   Early English Vaulting

required an enormous quantity of boarding for a cathedral.
There was plenty of timber in England in those days; but its
preparation into boards must have been costly, since it was all
cut up by hand. So the thirteenth-century builders used centering for their ribs only—the spaces in between are called the

117

cells, and these were filled in with carefully shaped stones (voutains), slightly arched from rib to rib. To do this, a cleverly expanding mould was used, which could be drawn out; for, starting from the bottom, the cell became wider as the building progressed upwards(*67*, 1–2).

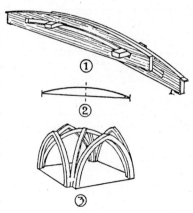

A great saving of weight was effected, and consequently we find the supporting columns becoming lighter and more beautiful in appearance than those of Norman times.

67 1, 2, Expanding centering for vaults. 3, Ribs of a vault cell

Gaining in confidence, the thirteenth-century builders vaulted the naves of their churches as well as the aisles.

The slender columns, grouped around the larger one in the centre, should be noticed, with their collar-like mouldings in the middle, and more delicately carved and moulded caps. The same features were attached to the narrow lancet-shaped windows which took the place of the semicircular-shaped tops of the Norman period. Stained glass was now used in church windows. The arches to the nave were far more deeply moulded than before. When anything is peculiarly beautiful, depending for its general result on just proportion and an absolute fitness for purpose, rather than on useless ornament, we say that it is Greek in idea. Early English was the Greek period of Gothic architecture. Westminster Abbey and Salisbury Cathedral, to mention two examples, are absolutely satisfying in their wonderful beauty and simplicity. There is nothing involved or difficult; very little ornament; no tricks are played; yet the result is far finer than many later examples of a much richer character.

This might be said as well of the general life of the people: the end of the thirteenth century closed the best period of the real Middle Ages. Men and women were still fairly contented. The Black Death and social discontent were still a long way off.

68   A Manor-House of the time of Edward I
Based on Aydon Castle, Northumberland ("Early English" style)

THE MANOR-HOUSE

Fig. *68* shows a thirteenth-century manor-house built in Edward I's reign; but, although more attention has been paid to comfort, it still closely resembles the house we described when we were dealing with the twelfth century. Indeed, this type of house-building, of which the central feature was the hall, remained in favour among English architects until the beginning of the seventeenth century. Naturally, there were many changes and improvements; but almost all the houses built were elaborations of the same idea.

The main living-rooms of the house are on what we should now call the first floor; and if the reader consults the plan he will notice that you have to go up steps at 1, to reach the front door at 2, which leads into a space screened off at the end of the hall—this latter, 3, including the screens, is about 40 feet long by 25 feet wide; a fine big place for a small house. The hall has no rooms above it, and has a timbered roof and, though on a smaller scale, it was finished off in much the same way, and

119

served the same purposes, as that described on page 111. On the right-hand side, by the front entrance, is the door to the kitchen, 4 on plan, with a cellar under it, and another room over. In old manuscripts, servants are often shown going up ladders indoors; so there may have been a ladder up to this room over the kitchen. At Stokesay Castle, which is also of the thirteenth century, there is a ladder-like staircase at this end of the hall, leading to a room in a similar position and this would have given access to a gallery over the screens at the entrance. In one of Henry III's many instructions to the keepers of his houses, he orders that a trap-door and ladder down to a room be taken away and a staircase made; and, if monarchs put up with ladders, their subjects would have done so too. The solar, or withdrawing-room, for the use of the lord, is at 5; and probably a chapel was contrived here, by internal partitions which have now disappeared. At Little Wenham Hall, in Suffolk, a splendid thirteenth-century brick house, there is a most beautiful chapel; for a chapel was always included in a house of any size. There would probably have been a wardrobe here as well, where clothes could be made and mended, and the jewellery and plate stored. At 6 is the washing and lavatory accommodation. Baths began to be used in the time of Edward I, and are supposed to have been introduced by his Spanish wife, Eleanor of Castile.

The rooms on the ground floor were no doubt used as

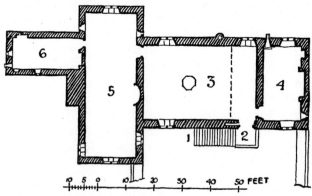

69   Plan of the Manor-House shown as fig. 68

1 Steps	4 The Kitchen
2 Front Door	5 Solar or Withdrawing-Room
3 Hall	6 Washing or Lavatory Accommodation

70　A Page from a Missal written and illuminated for Lesnes Abbey, Erith, Kent, about 1200

In the Victoria and Albert Museum

71 "Sumer is icumen in" (about 1225)

This song is a round, the cross marking the point at which each fresh voice enters. Readers can pick out the tune on the piano if they will remember that the C clef is used, the first note thus being F (above middle C). The diamond-shaped notes are quavers, the others crotchets. On the word "in", play three quavers, and on the "cu" syllable of the third "cuc cu" in the fourth line play a crotchet and a quaver. The part marked "pes" is not part of the tune, but a continuous bass, repeated as often as desired.

In the British Museum

barracks for the retainers, and also as a store place for the large quantities of food needed to carry the household through the winter.

The entrance is defended by an inner bailey, with battlemented walls around; and outside this is an outer bailey, surrounded by another wall, which would have enclosed the stables, granaries, and workshops for making weapons and farm tools.

In this house we see the effects of Edward I's strong domestic policy. Now that life was becoming secure, men could afford to build houses that, despite their fortified walls, were more like homes and less like castles.

Stokesay Castle in Shropshire is a well-preserved thirteenth-century manor-house, slightly defended by moat, gatehouse —rebuilt in the Elizabethan period—and tower; the curtain walls have disappeared. The great hall dates from 1240; the tower is, unexpectedly, a half-century later; Lawrence of Ludlow, a rich merchant, got his licence to crenellate or fortify in 1290. There are rooms at both ends of the Great Hall; the unusual wooden staircase leads to the rooms in the overhanging half-timber addition of c. 1620; the solar near the tower, with its elaborate seventeenth-century fittings, is reached by an outside stair.

FURNITURE AND HOME-LIFE

The illustration (72) is of a solar such as would have been found in the thirteenth-century manor-house that we are describing. Here the lord and lady of the house slept, received their friends, and enjoyed any little privacy that there was to be had in the reign of Edward I; and there was not very much —people of every condition, from king to peasant, still lived together in close proximity like rabbits in a warren. The king himself, surrounded by courtiers and attendants, was very seldom left alone.

In the stone-built fireplace great logs burnt on the open hearth, from which the ashes were rarely cleared away. The furniture consisted of heavy chairs like church stalls, chests for storing precious possessions, and forms. At the right-hand side of the fireplace is shown a perch, used to hang up clothes. Window seats were generally provided, and must have made a pretty and useful addition to the rather scanty furnishing. The

72   A Solar, or Withdrawing-Room ("Early English" Style)

window itself is not glazed, as glass was a rarity only found in the king's palace or the wealthier monasteries; a little piece, however, might be introduced into the trefoil at the top. The larger openings would be protected by irons bars on the out-side, and wooden shutters within. On a cold or wet day, if you wanted light, you must also let in the wind and weather. Smoke, puffed out from the fire by strong draughts, would have helped to make the room additionally cheerless.

Carpets began to come into use, and, like baths, were introduced into England by Eleanor of Castile. Matthew Paris, a chronicler of the period, talking of the Spanish Ambassadors who preceded her arrival, says:

> The manners of the Spaniards were utterly at variance with English customs and habits; that while the walls of their lodgings in the Temple were hung with silk and tapestry, and the very floors covered with costly carpets, their retinue was vulgar and disorderly; that they had few horses and many mules.

The Crusades, too, may have helped to popularise carpets; for Crusaders, returning from the East, would almost certainly have brought back the beautiful rugs that had been manufactured there from the earliest times; while merchants, coming to the great English fairs, and finding a demand for carpets, would begin to import them.

As to the decorations of the walls of the solar, we discover in the Liberate Rolls of Henry III much evidence of his love of colour, and learn the names of the artists he employed. The sheriff of Wiltshire is commanded to carry out certain alterations to the king's chapel at Clarendon, and

> wainscote the king's lower chamber, and to paint that wainscote of a green colour, and to put a border to it, and to cause the heads of kings and queens to be painted on the borders; and to paint on the walls of the king's upper chamber the story of St. Margaret Virgin, and the four Evangelists; and to paint the wainscote of the same chamber of a green colour, spotted with gold, and to paint on it heads of men and women; and all these paintings are to be done with good and exquisite colours.

Again, Edward Fitz-Otho, keeper of the king's works at Westminster, is ordered to "raise the chimney of the queen's chamber, and to paint the chimney of the chamber aforesaid, and on it cause to be pourtrayed a figure of Winter, which as well by its sad countenance as by other miserable distortions of the body may be deservedly likened to Winter itself".

The roof of our solar is worth consideration, for it gives a

73, 74 Little Wenham Hall, Suffolk, from the South-East.
Garderobe block restored. *Below*, Plan of the Hall

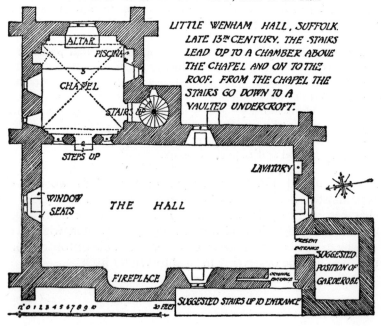

LITTLE WENHAM HALL, SUFFOLK.
LATE 13ᵗʰ CENTURY. THE STAIRS
LEAD UP TO A CHAMBER ABOVE
THE CHAPEL AND ON TO THE
ROOF. FROM THE CHAPEL THE
STAIRS GO DOWN TO A
VAULTED UNDERCROFT.

ALTAR
PISCINA
CHAPEL
STAIRS UP
STEPS UP
WINDOW SEATS
THE HALL
LAVATORY
PRESENT ENTRANCE
SUGGESTED POSITION OF GARDEROBE
ORIGINAL ENTRANCE
FIREPLACE
SUGGESTED STAIRS UP TO ENTRANCE
20 FEET

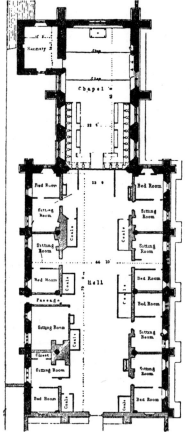

75 Plan of St. Mary's Hospital, Chichester

type of early timbered roof adapted to a steep pitch, instead of the flatter one shown over the hall on page 112. There is the same tie-beam; but the king-post standing on it is taller and is tenoned at the top into a beam running lengthways, across which, in their turn, rest the collars of the roof framed in between the rafters.

Figs. *73* and *74* explain the details of Little Wenham Hall, in Suffolk, to which we have already referred. The kitchen here was probably a separate building in the bailey. The colour of Little Wenham is one of its greatest charms. It is the first medieval brick building. The Romans had been great brick builders; the Anglo-Saxons liked timber framing; the Normans built in stone and concrete. Here at Wenham bricks were used once more: a rather thinner

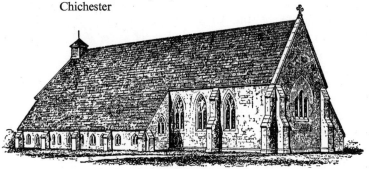

76 St. Mary's Hospital, Chichester

127

brick than those of to-day, and varying in colour from bright yellow through all the reds to plum colours and blacks.

Next we include a plan and view of St. Mary's Hospital, Chichester(75, 76), which retains many of the features of a medieval refuge for the aged. It was built during Edward I's reign, about 1290, and the hall with its fine timber pillars is like a church nave, the chapel with its stalls and good screen being placed like a chancel. The divisions which form the apartments are in brick, of 1680, probably replacing earlier wooden partitions. The little rooms are very small but snug, and the old inmates have an allowance, with medical attendance, coal and faggots. Originally, wood, to be chopped on the hall floor, was provided.

Fig. 77 shows a jug, in the collection of medieval pottery at the British Museum. It is rather odd that, during the Middle Ages, pottery did not keep pace with the other crafts, probably because it was only used by the humbler folk, and the rich people used metal vessels, as shown in fig. 115 in the fourteenth-century chapter.

You can also see at the British Museum specimens of the floor tiles, inlaid with patterns, that were used in the Middle Ages and can still be found in churches to-day. We have shown some of these tiles in fig. 78. They seem at first to have been manufactured almost entirely by monks, who now and then let their fancy run away with them; for we are told that a statute of the Cistercian Order, in 1265, rebuked the Abbot of Beaubec "for having for a long time allowed his monks to construct for persons not belonging to the Order, pavements that exhibit levity and curiosity".

The fertility of design and play of fancy in these floor tiles is amazing; the examples given

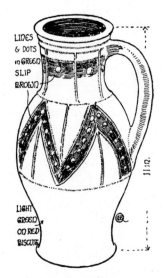

77 A Jug
(*From the British Museum*)

128

78 Patterns of Tile Paving from Westminster Abbey. (*From a drawing by Miss E. Matley Moore*)

(fig. *78*) are from Westminster Abbey. They were made in little beehive ovens, the pattern being impressed in the soft red clay, and yellow clay being run into it as a fluid paste. The tile was then fired, being glazed all over or only on the pattern.

Malvern was one of the greatest centres from which tiles were distributed. It is interesting, therefore, that Mr. Charlton of the Historical Monuments Commission has discovered a thirteenth-century tile kiln at Clarendon Palace near Salisbury, at one time a hunting-box and, later, a country house of some of England's medieval rulers. This is the first secular English kiln of which we have any record.

Fig. *79* shows an aumbry, or cupboard, from Chester Cathedral. The very beautiful wrought-iron scroll work was applied to the face of the boarded doors, and made them stronger and safer from thieves. The ironwork is not connected with the hinge straps, as it is on one of the porch doors at Eaton Bray, in Bedfordshire. The ironwork here is supposed to have been the work of Thomas de Leghtone, who made the Eleanor grille in Westminster Abbey in 1294. It is thought that Thomas was of Leighton Buzzard, since the ironwork in the doors of the parish church there, and at Turvey, is all of the same rare type, and all three places are quite close together. It is called stamped work, because the terminations of the scrolls were formed by hammering the hot iron into metal dies. This looks as if

79   A Thirteenth-Century Aumbry or Cupboard,
from Chester Cathedral

they had discovered how to make steel, or chilled iron, for the
dies.

THE FISHING INDUSTRY

England has always been a maritime nation, and the fish
round her coasts have furnished the English people with food
from time immemorial. An amusing eleventh-century illustration
shows a man in a very small boat, with a very large rod rather
like the bough of a tree, and a very thick line, hooking a fish
out of the water, while other fish are swimming away in alarm.

130

Entries in the Domesday Book show rents from herring fishing round the coast. Yarmouth was a great centre of the herring industry, and herrings were brought ashore, salted and packed in barrels. These barrels were slung over packhorses and taken off to be sold.

We must remember the lack of cold storage and the difficulty of keeping fresh fish, which would account for the vast amount eaten salted; and it is thought that, when deep-sea fishing, the ships had some kind of well in which to keep the fish alive. Cod and ling were plentiful and well known; and sturgeons, whales, and porpoises were considered a delicacy; while, in 1237, Rye and Winchelsea supplied the King's Court with whiting and plaice. We hear a great deal about eels (p. 68); and eel traps, made of wicker, like long lobster traps, were placed in rivers. Judging by the Domesday Book, eels were plentiful, and we read of fisheries yielding thousands every year.

Nets were in general use, the size of the mesh regulated by law; and, although there is no mention of a fisherman's gild, the industry was carefully regulated. Dues were exacted by the king and his various officers and by port authorities; prices were regulated; and stringent measures were taken against regrators and all those who tried to corner the market or to deal in fish unfairly, to the detriment of the citizen customer.

COUNTRY LIFE

So far as country life was concerned, there were no very marked changes in agricultural conditions in the thirteenth century, except that, as time went on, the methods of farming improved, and the villein was winning his way towards freedom. As civilisation progressed, the lords began to feel the need of money to purchase luxuries; and it became more and more the custom to take money payments from the villeins, as rent for the use of their holdings, instead of part of their labour and pro- duce. Then, with the growth of sheep-farming, fewer men were needed on the land; so that it was often convenient for the lord to allow the villein to purchase his freedom by the payment of a fine, leaving him in the position of a labourer, free to travel about, and hire himself to anyone needing help, or go to the towns and obtain work there. But the nobles still held the land, and farmed their own demesne. The manors were self-supporting, or nearly so, the lords and their dependants growing all the wheat and meat they required; making their own bread, butter, and cheese; wearing homespun clothes woven on their own looms, and, in fact, buying little outside, except tar, fish, furs, salt, iron, spices, silks, and fine cloths at the great fairs.

We gather from various writers of the thirteenth century that each manor-house possessed a walled-in garden, carefully tended, in which were grown flowers, herbs, vegetables, and fruit for the owner's use. Nut trees were cultivated for the oil they yielded. Cabbages, peas and beans, beetroots, onions, garlic, and leeks are all mentioned, as well as lettuce, watercress, and hops. For flowers, we read of the rose, lily, sunflower, violet and poppy, and also of the gillyflower or clove-pink; and in the fourteenth century Chaucer speaks of flowers thus:

> There sprange the vyolet al newe,
> And fresshe pervynké [periwinkle] rich of hewe,
> And floures yelowe, white, and rede,
> Suche plenté grewe there never in mede.

Each garden would have its well, or pond, stocked with fish; and in the Liberate Rolls of Henry III the bailiff of Kennington is commanded to make a haye, or hedge, at the causeway at the head of the pool of the king's stew, in the park there.

The bailiff of Woodstock is also ordered to build two good and high walls around our queen's garden, and make a becoming and fair "herbour" near our vivary, in which the same queen may walk.

80 A Well

Bees were kept, since honey was used for nearly all sweetening purposes. It is mentioned in the Domesday Book, and an Anglo-Norman manuscript contains a very amusing picture of bee-keepers and their hives.

As we have already noted, the Lords of the Manor farmed their own demesne, which was under the jurisdiction of a steward. Working under the steward was the bailiff, or steward's

132

81   Washing Hands
(*See also fig. 63*)

foreman, and below him came the reeve, who was elected by the peasants themselves and shared out the work of the farm among them. On his honesty and fair-dealing much of their happiness depended; and in the *Luttrell Psalter* we see the reapers working away at the direction of his outstretched wand. Under him, again, were the hayward, who was responsible for the hedges, the swineherd, cowherd, dairymaid, and the foreman of the mowers. The mills, as we have said, belonged to the Lord of the Manor, whether monastery or landowner. These mills were let to millers who, in return for grinding, kept a portion of the corn they received. There was also a village bakery under the same ownership, where the villagers could bake their bread. The village meeting-place was the church, which, if not attached to a monastery, was built by the Lord of the Manor.

In the church was transacted much of the village business. It was even used as a bank, and the villagers deposited within its walls any deeds or money that they feared to keep in their own small houses. The parish priest, appointed by the Lord of the Manor, was given a house, a gield or glebe, and a tenth portion of each parishioner's stock. For his part, he was bound to keep his church in repair, to have always by him a small sum to help the poor and needy, and to give hospitality to passing travellers.

82   Tubbing

133

The great high roads still followed
the direction of the old Roman high-
ways, and many led through large
tracts of forest land, which were
infested with bands of robbers and
outlaws of all kinds. The abbots of
St. Albans provided armed men to
patrol the road between that city and
London, for the greater safety of
travellers thereon. Such was the
terror that these highway robbers
inspired.

83   Digging with a
wooden spade

In 1285 a law was passed
which decreed that all high roads
between large market towns were to be widened, so that
no bushes, trees, or ditches remained within 200 feet of each
side of the road. Landowners who refused thus to clear
their land were held responsible for any robberies committed there.

Many Cistercian monasteries were built in the twelfth and
thirteenth centuries, largely in those areas that had been
devastated by the Conqueror in his wasting of the north;
and the monks brought the land back into cultivation. The
Cistercians were also largely responsible for the development
of sheep-breeding. As we have explained in our account of
monastic life in the twelfth century, all the monastic orders
engaged in farming and were keenly interested in the manage-
ment of their estates, introducing numerous improvements,
which the barons adopted during times of peace. The same
odium attached to trade as in Abbot Samson's time: to borrow
money was considered thriftless; to lend it, usury.

WATER-MILLS

Our next illustration (*84*) is of one of the oldest types of construction in Old England, or for that matter in the world's
history—a water-mill. We have already described how, in the
twelfth century, Abbot Samson ordered a Dean Herbert to
demolish a mill built without his consent, although it is not
clear whether it was a water- or a windmill. In the Liberate
Rolls of Henry III there are instructions to the sheriff of Surrey

and Sussex about various building works that are to be carried
out at "our hall at Guildford", and he is further instructed to
"build three mills in the park, to wit, one for hard corn,
another for malt, and a third for fulling". Again, there is
nothing to indicate which type of mill is to be built. There is
an illustration of a windmill in the so-called *Windmill Psalter*
of the late thirteenth century. It is of the post type illustrated

84   A Water-Mill

in fig. *131*, as also is that shown in fig. *127*. Certainly water-mills have been used from the very earliest times; man very quickly set about using some energy other than his own to grind corn—the hand-mill was hard work. The Egyptians used water-mills, and a very early form of mill resembled a small paddle-steamer moored in midstream, the current of the river turning the paddles, which operated a shaft connected to the mill-stones inside the boat. Similar devices can still be seen on some of the rivers of Southern Europe.

Now as to the principle on which a water-mill works. The first thing to do is to select a site on a river where the requisite head of water can be obtained, and by head is meant the fall of the river. A very placid, slowly moving stream, though it may give more continuous results, involves unnecessary labour. The oldest type of wheel is that called the overshot, because the water turns it by shooting over the top. For this purpose, the river must be tapped some distance away, and the water brought down in a leat to the mill-pond, which acts as a store; from the pond it is led to the top of the wheel, through a sort of channel called the head-race. This is shown in our illustration (*84*), which is of the simplest form of overshot wheel, as a wooden trough with a sluice at one end, operated by a cog on a shaft turned by a handle inside the mill. So long as the sluice is closed, the water goes to waste through the shoot at the side; but if the sluice is raised, the overflow is at once stopped, a jet of water being discharged from the bottom of the sluice over the top of the wheel. It will be noticed that the wheel is constructed so as to form what are called buckets, which are full as the wheel goes down, but empty as it comes up; thus the weight of the water plus the force of the jet keeps the wheel turning. The speed of the wheel can be regulated by the amount of water allowed to escape from under the sluice. The water falls away at the bottom into what is called the tail-race, and joins the river at a lower level. Now it is evident that, if full power is to be derived from the wheel, it must be kept clear of the water in the tail-race, or the resistance of this water to the turning movement of the wheel would mean loss of power. A good head of water regulates the size of your wheel, which itself determines the amount of leverage, or power, exerted on the axle. The latter is continued as a shaft through the wall of the mill and so drives the mill-stones. This part of the work is the same in a water-mill as a windmill; and the operation of grinding is described on page 246 in our chapter on the fifteenth century. The undershot wheel is operated in the same way as the early mills, which were said to be like paddle-steamers—the water is let out of a sluice so that it is discharged on to the bottom of the wheel. The old water-mill is worth studying, since it was the forerunner of the modern water turbine; but that is another story.

GAMES AND MUSIC

Our ancestors did not believe in the gospel of all work and no play, perhaps because they had seen its results; and we find that in the Middle Ages men and women played many games that now belong to children alone. It must be remembered that travelling was both slow and dangerous, and visiting, therefore, not to be lightly undertaken. Books were very few and not within the reach of many. At home, during the evenings, various occupations and amusements served to pass the time, and singing was one of them. We know this, because, in a miraculous way, a thirteenth-century song has come down to us—"Sumer is icumen in", composed about 1225. Fig. *71* shows the original score, preserved in the British Museum. This is the oldest known harmonised music still performed to-day. We are indebted to Mr. A. Forbes Milne for the selection of songs given here and in other chapters.

The ladies did good work with their needles, and many exquisite pieces of embroidery were produced at this period. The men might have their bows or other weapons to mend or sharpen, or they played at chess or tables, the latter being really the game of backgammon. Draughts were played, and fig. *85*

85   An Ivory Draughtsman (full size).
Early Thirteenth-Century
(*British Museum*)

shows a beautiful thirteenth-century ivory draughtsman from the British Museum.

86   A Performing Bear

Sometimes a pilgrim, journeying to or from some shrine, would seek shelter for the night, and would enliven the company with tales of his travels or other stories that he had gathered by the way.

Strolling players too, minstrels and jugglers, moved from place to place, always sure of a welcome, and of their bed and board, if they had aught to show or do that would help to break the monotony of the hours when daylight had gone.

Travellers depended largely on manors and monasteries for their night's lodging. No taverns that offered regular shelter for the night are known before the fourteenth century. In the thirteenth century and before, we read of ale-houses and cook-shops; but sleeping accommodation was haphazard. Then temporary shelters began to be erected for travellers round the

87   Hoodman Blind

88 A leaf from a Psalter by William de Brailes of scenes in the lives
of Adam and Eve and Cain and Abel, Mid-Thirteenth Century

In the Fitzwilliam Museum, Cambridge

89　A Fourteenth-Century Hall

ale-houses or cook-shops; the inns of universities and inns of court started as a collection of poor lodgings for scholars clustered round a common kitchen and hall.

At a very early period we read of games of ball, and of skipping. "Hoodman blind" seems also to have been a favourite. All these were played by grown-ups; "Hoodman blind", as will be seen in the illustration(87), was the forerunner of "blind-man's buff".

One of the players is blinded by his capuchon, or hood, being turned back to front, while his fellows, holding their hoods in their hands, try to hit him without being caught themselves. Sometimes, in old manuscripts, the capuchons are shown knotted, so as to give a sounder smack; and it can be taken for granted that all games were very much rougher than they are nowadays.

Dancing, too, was very popular, and we read a great deal of the "Carol", which would be more or less equivalent to our "Country-dances" of to-day.

JOUSTS AND TOURNAMENTS

Then there were games that helped to teach the art of warfare. Fighting, and the use of the lance, sword, and mace, must, like every other science, be taught and practised to attain any degree of perfection; and combats as a pastime became general in the Middle Ages, in order that young knights, in friendly

90   A Combat

tests of skill and strength, might learn to bear themselves well on the battlefield.

Various rules were laid down for these combats, which gradually became, as jousts and tournaments, occasions of great pomp and ceremony, with fixed rules for each part of the programme.

Tourneys were combats between two equally matched parties of knights. Before the fray, each knight had to vow solemnly that he entered the fight only as an exercise of arms, and not to satisfy any private quarrel. Despite these precautions, the combat often became a fight to the death; and we read how, at one tournament in 1240, sixty knights were killed, some being choked by the dust and others crushed to death by the horses in the mêlée.

Sir Walter Scott's *Ivanhoe* contains a very interesting account of a tournament at which Prince John was present. In 1274 Edward I, with his knights, took part in a tournament at Chalôns, against the Comte de Chalôns and some Burgundian nobles. Here the fray became so heated that several of the combatants were killed. The Popes tried from time to time to put an end to these tournaments, but without success.

Fig. *90* shows two knights engaged in a friendly encounter. Their armour is that of the late thirteenth century. Notice the heavy and rather clumsy helmets, and the banded mail that they wear, covered with a surcoat, but with no steel plates on either arms or legs. These were not worn until later. In the fifteenth-century chapter an illustration is given of a joust (*173*).

DECORATION

Our illumination of the thirteenth century (*88*) is from a Psalter by William de Brailes, a great English illuminator who used sometimes to sign his work. Only six precious leaves of this masterpiece have come down to us; and here he depicts scenes from the stories of Adam and Eve and Cain and Abel. In the page of the Last Judgment Brailes has drawn himself, seized by a strong angel from the mouth of Hell (*91*). How we wish an angel with a great sword were ready to snatch a poor artist or writer from the bankruptcy court or a tax-defaulter's prison, or stand between him and his worries and follies!

To conclude our chapter on the thirteenth century, we include a tail-piece illustrating the characteristic ornament of the Early English period. We have seen how in Norman times

91 An angel snatches from wrath
William de Brailes, identified by
his signature

the decoration showed traces of the acanthus scroll of the Romans; thirteenth-century craftsmen carried on the same idea and perfected it. All their curves and lines are beautiful, and the ruggedness of the Norman age has disappeared. The details of this pattern, and variations of it, were used in capitals to the columns, for the carved corbels supporting vaulting shafts, and in many other ways; and, with the dog-tooth ornament inserted in the arch mouldings, and the diaper pattern incised on the plain wall surfaces, it made up almost the whole range of patterning used in the thirteenth century. Early English architecture is so beautifully proportioned in itself, the mouldings have such true outlines, and the quality of the workmanship is so excellent, that it does not seem to call for much ornamentation.

In our twelfth-century chapter we tried to explain how all ornament and pattern has a foundation of structural lines, rather like the bones in a human body. It may sound foolish to talk of beauty of line; a line is, well, just a line. This may be true enough if the line is straight; but let your lines be curved and, the combinations of curves being endless, you get beauty, or ugliness, as a result of your skill, or lack of it. The reader should experiment on his own account: inventing patterns is great fun. Find the idea, and the structural line on which a design is built up; graft a variation on it, and see what happens.

92 "Early English" Ornament

143

Dates.	Kings and Queens of England and France.	Famous Men.	Great Events, Sea Fights, and Land Battles.	Principal Buildings (B., Benedictine ; C., Cistercian).
1300	Edward I. and *Philip IV.*		Start of Border Wars with Scotland, which last till 1550	Exeter Choir, 1291–1307
1305			Captivity of the Popes, 1305–78 ; and death of William Wallace, 1305	
1306		Robert Bruce crowned		
1307	Edward II., *m.* Isabella of France			Exeter Nave, 1308–50
1310		Piers Gaveston		Winchelsea Church, 1310
1311				
1314	*Louis X.*		Lords Ordainers	
1315			Battle of Bannockburn	
1316	*Philip V.*		Famine	
			Lancaster, and rise of De-spensers	Wells Chapter-House, 1319
1321				Beverley Nave, 1320–49
				Ely Octagon, Choir, and Lady Chapel, B., 1321–49
1322	*Charles IV.*		Battle of Boroughbridge	
			Execution of Thomas of Lancaster	
1325			Queen obtains French help	
1327	Edward III., *m.* Philippa of Hainault			
1328	*Philip VI.*			
1330			Flemings settle in Norwich and start English manu-facture	Wells Choir
1333			Battle of Halidon Hill	
1334				Salisbury Spire, C.
1338			Start of Hundred Years War with France, 1338–1453	
1340			Sea fight off Sluys	
1341				Penshurst
1342				Queen's College, Oxford
1346			Battles of Crécy and Ne-ville's Cross	Winchester Presbytery, 1345–66
1347			Capture of Calais	
1348			Black Death, 1348–49	
1349			Statute of Labourers	
1350	*John the Good*			Winchester Nave, B., 1371–1460, and west end of Westminster Abbey Nave, B., 1350–1420
1351		William Langland		
1356			Battle of Poitiers	Edington Choir, 1352–61
1360		Geoffrey Chaucer, 1340–1400		
1361			Peace of Bretigny	
1364	*Charles V.*			
1366		Froissart, 1337–1410		Gloucester North Transept, 1368–73
1367			Battle of Navarette	
1369			Renewal of French War	Black Prince's Chantry, Canterbury, 1370–9
1370		William of Wykeham	Storm of Limoges	
1371				Warwick Castle, 1371
1373		John Wyclif and the Lollards, 1324–84	English translation of Bible	
1374			Loss of Aquitaine	
1376		Black Prince dies	Good Parliament	
1377	Richard II., *m.* (1) Anne of Bohemia ; (2) Isa-bella of France	Brunelleschi, 1377–1446		
1378			Captivity of Popes ended	Canterbury Nave, 1379–1400, C.
			The Schism, 1378–1415	
1379		John of Gaunt		
1380	*Charles VI.*			York Choir, 1380–1400
1381			Wat Tyler's Rebellion	
1382				Winchester School
1386		Donatello, 1386–1466		Bodiam Castle
1387				New College, Oxford
1396			Truce with France	
1399	Henry IV., *m.* (1) Mary Bohun ; (2) Joanna of Navarre.		Richard abdicates	Westminster Hall, 1397–9

93   Chart of the "Decorated" Period of Design, from 1300 to 1399

94   A Knight of the time of Richard II

Chapter III

FOURTEENTH CENTURY

THE fourteenth century opened with the fairest prospects. Edward I's long reign was drawing to a close, and his wise government had produced settled and peaceful conditions. Yet this fateful century was destined to be one of great misery, and to see important changes in the mode of English life. It was a case of the unexpected happening; for, during the thirteenth century, all the omens had appeared to be favourable. At the beginning of the century, John had been forced to sign Magna Charta; Henry III was finally brought to book by Simon de Montfort, and his Parliament carried on the same idea of freedom from oppression. The Church, which had become rich and slothful, was subjected to the reforming influence of the Friars, who came in 1221. Edward I almost succeeded in uniting the whole island under one crown, and concerned himself with improving home conditions rather than with waging war abroad. In fact, he then possessed only Gascony, and was not to be tempted into useless knight-errantry. The Statute of

145

95   Carrying Babies

Winchester was passed, which compelled all men to help in keeping the peace. Edward's motto was "Pactum serva" (Keep troth), and well he did it. "The Hammer of the Scots" was perhaps a hard man, but at the same time he was a great king.

But with the French Wars of Edward III, which lasted with brief intervals for 100 years (1338–1453), came a fresh wave of social restlessness, and once again the clouds grew dark. Then, in the middle of the century, the terrible Black Death broke out, a plague that helped ultimately to destroy the whole structure of the feudal system.

Fortunately, in the poems of Chaucer and William Langland, we have a lively picture of the middle classes and the working people; while, by contrast, the valiant knights and their doughty and chivalrous deeds live for us in the vivid pages of Froissart and other chroniclers. There was much glamour in knighthood; but warfare, as it always has been, was sordid and terrible. We can obtain a vivid impression both of the glory of chivalry and of the everyday life of humdrum ordinary folk from the splendid MSS. of this century, when the art of illumination reached perhaps its highest level. Many of these great works of art have come down to us, and they represent the patient efforts of accomplished scribes over a number of laborious years.

In spite of its darker sides, there was much that was splendid about the fourteenth century. It was an age of romance and chivalry, when architecture became ornate and elaborate; and we can see from such buildings as Exeter and Beverley something of its luxuriant grandeur, which was cut short by the coming of the distinctive, but sterner, Perpendicular style, as it spread from the quire of Gloucester soon after the middle of the century.

Less spectacular, but more vital, was the rise of the merchant class, who were increasing in influence and importance, and organising themselves as an active, sturdy burgher class in the cities. The wool trade was of immense importance during our period; and the export of fish, metalwork, honey, and other goods also brought in large profits. The fourteenth century was a period of rapid change and development; the England of Richard II was a vastly different place from the England of Edward I.

COSTUME

We must now consider how these changes were reflected in the everyday things of the time; and, as we did when discussing the thirteenth century, will begin with a description of the costume of the people.

We have seen how beautiful was the simplicity of dress in the thirteenth century, how useful was each garment, and yet how graceful was the whole in its severity of line and fold. In the fourteenth century this simplicity and grace gave place to greater richness of detail and general extravagance of effect, until, in the fifteenth century, many of the garments became quite grotesque, neither allowing any freedom of movement to their wearers nor possessing any grace of their own.

Our first figure in fig. *98*, a young man, shows how the form of the tunic, or cotte, was changing. This cotte has now become shorter and less flowing; indeed, it rather resembles a coat, for it is buttoned all down the front, and fits the figure tightly. In this form it was called the "cotte hardie", and was often worn, especially on horseback, without any surcoat or over-garment. The sleeves were buttoned from elbow to wrist.

Notice, too, now there is no longer any need to confine the folds of the tunic into the waist, that the belt has been slipped down until it is low on the hips. These belts were richly jewelled, and carried a long dagger, often of exquisite workmanship. The chaperon was still worn; this young man's is hanging down behind; and the cape round his shoulders is ornamented by being cut up at

96   A Bird-cage Seller

147

97   Spinning

"Deceite weeping, spinning God
hath given
To women kindly while they
may liven"
(Chaucer's prologue on
"Wife of Bath")

the hem into long strips. His hat is of dark felt, and fastened in the front of the crown is a beautiful jewelled brooch. His shoes are more pointed than those of thirteenth-century men, and all the colours in his clothing are more gay.

The cotte of a lady of this period retains much of its old shape, except that the skirt is rather fuller, and the bodice more closely fitting. This lady's belt, like that of the man, now rests round her hips and not her waist. The bliaut has quite given place to the surcoat. She wears a surcoat, which is still really not unlike a bliaut, although it is lower in the neck and larger round the arm-holes, and generally looser. At this time furs were worn separately over the surcoat, and it was not until the fifteenth century that they became part of the garment itself.

As for her hair, it is very elaborately dressed, and worn in jewelled plaits turned up on either side of the face. Her head is encircled by a jewelled band, so rich as almost to have the effect of a small crown. Some women wore their hair in golden nets which quite covered the head; and some again, more especially if elderly or in mourning, still wore the coiffe and wimple of linen round the face and neck. Women's shoes were little different from those of men.

The second lady wears a pelisse, with a large, straight collar of fur. This pelisse is fastened down the front with little buttons, and hangs in long, full folds, and is an outdoor garment, cut full to go easily over the cotte and surcoat. The sleeves are curious, hanging in the same way as those of the scholar in the thirteenth century. Her hair is somewhat differently dressed,

148

98 Costume of the "Decorated" Period. Fourteenth Century

and has a long curl; but she wears the same type of jewelled circlet as her friend.

Perhaps you may not at once have guessed that the strange headgear worn by the old gentleman is, in fact, a capuchon. This was still used in its original shape for travelling, and in stormy weather; but in towns and among fashionable folk it had been so turned and twisted as to be scarcely recognisable.

This man has drawn over the crown of his head the opening originally intended for his face, and then has twisted all the rest of the hood around like a turban, the scalloped end of the cape sticking out at the top like a cockscomb.

He wears a surcoat. Notice that it is cut rather differently from the one in the thirteenth century, and is a good deal fuller in the skirt, also that the sleeves are longer and more pointed, and that it fastens right up to the throat. This surcoat is made of some richly brocaded material, and is lined with fur. There was an odd custom at the time of wearing one sleeve of the cotte hanging far over the hand, while the other was of normal length. This man has one such sleeve.

The last man of this illustration shows how the general character of the armour is changing and developing. The coat of mail, or hauberk, had been found to give insufficient protection, and efforts were made to render it more effective by means of plates of steel on the arms and legs and feet. The hands also were now encased in steel gauntlets. This knight's helmet is much less cumbersome than those of the thirteenth century; it is more like a conical cap without a visor. His surcoat, now fitting tightly over his hauberk, is emblazoned with his coat of arms.

The little page next to him carries his "tourney" helmet, or as it was generally called, "the heaume", which, being as heavy and cumbersome as it was gorgeous, was only used at tournaments or on great occasions. Pages at this time wore their master's badge

99 Drummers

151

across the front of their tunics. They were the sons of well-to-do parents, and, when quite young, were sent to live in the house of some noble, who, in return for their services, had them educated with his own sons by the household priest.

One noticeable feature in the armour of this century was the advent of chain mail. Until now banded mail had been most commonly worn—that is to say, mail composed of rings of steel sewn on to stout linen or velvet. These rings were held in place by pipings of the material being drawn up in between. (A fuller explanation of this mail is found in the account of thirteenth-century armour, p. 93.)

Chain mail was made of rings of steel interwoven one with the other, without any groundwork of velvet or linen. It was, of course, much lighter and more flexible than banded mail, but was nearly always worn over a gambeson, a quilted garment, a kind of thick tunic well padded with wool, used merely to give extra protection under the armour. Chain mail is generally supposed to have been brought to England by the Crusaders from the East, where it had been in use for a very long time.

Chaucer, in his "Tale of Sir Thopas", gives us an interesting description of a young knight and his armour:

> And next his sherte an akétoun [quilted linen tunic or
>   gambeson],
> And over that an haubergeoun [breast-plate]
> For percygne of his herte;
> And over that a fyn hawberk,
> Was al y-wrought of Jewés werk,
> Ful strong it was of plate;
> And over that his cote-armour [surcoat],
> As whit as is a lilye flour,
> In which he wol debate.
>
> His sheeld was al of gold so reed,
> And ther-inne was a borés [boar's] heed,
> A charbocle [carbuncle] bisyde;
> And there he swoor, on ale and breed,
> How that the geaunt [giant] shal be deed,
> "Bitydé what bityde!"
>
> His jambeaux [jambarts or leg pieces] were of quyrboilly
>   [cuir bouilli]

His swerdés shethe of yvory,
His helm of laton [brass] bright;
His sadel was of rewel boon [smooth bone];
His brydel as the sonné shoon,
Or as the mooné light.
His spere it was of fyn ciprees,
That bodeth werre [war], and no-thyng pees [peace],
The heed ful sharpe y-grounde;
His steedé was al dappull-gray,
It gooth an ambil in the way
Ful softély and rounde.

Another glimpse of masculine fashions is to be found in Chaucer's "Miller's Tale":

With Powlés wyndow corven on his shoes,
In hoes rede he wenté fetisly [neatly].

This mention of "Powlés wyndow", we are told, referred to the openwork tracery in fashionable shoes of the time, which resembled that of the great rose window at Old St. Paul's.

SHIP-BUILDING AND NAVAL WARFARE

Having seen what the people looked like, we will follow the same order as in the thirteenth-century chapter, and study the everyday things they used.

Fig. *100* illustrates a fourteenth-century ship, which shows several interesting developments. The hull is rather bluffer, and more tub-like, than that of the thirteenth century, and the fine lines of the older Viking boats are being lost. The body is raised up at stern and stem, and on the parts so raised beams are laid across, which form the floors to the castles, the sides being strengthened by cleats fastened on under the floor beams. Around the castles a sort of palisaded fence is built up as a protection, and these are more ship-like, and less castle-like, than those of the thirteenth century. The fronts of the castles towards the deck are closed in, with the result that comfortable cabins are formed for the sailors. Ladders from inside the cabins lead to the decks above. There is a big hawse-hole for the anchor cable, and the forestay is brought through this and fastened to the stem of the boat. The bowsprit has its bowline comb as in the century before, and rudders are now used instead of steering-oars.

100   A Fourteenth-Century Ship

The rigging of the ship remains much the same, with one mast and square sail; there were two-masted ships in the Mediterranean from very early times, but they were lateeners with leg-of-mutton sails, and until the fifteenth century they had no influence on British ship-design. It must have been in ships like the one we have illustrated that our men were carried to the French Wars.

Froissart gives an interesting account of the naval engagement of Sluys:

He (King Edward III) and his army sailed from the Thames, the day before the eve of St. John the Baptist, 1340, and made straight for Sluys. On his way he fell in with the French navy, of which we have been speaking, and though the numbers were four to one against him, resolved to give them battle. The French were equally desirous to engage, and as soon as they were within sight of the English, they filled the *Christopher*, the large ship which they had captured but a short time before, with trumpets and other warlike instruments, ordering her to begin the attack. The battle was fierce, murderous, and horrible. In the end the English came off victorious, the *Christopher* was recaptured by them, and all in her taken or killed.

154

THE DEVELOPMENT OF THE CASTLE

Writing of fights by sea reminds us of battles on land, and for the latter the castle was still necessary. Even though the Black Prince gained most of his victories by a superiority in manœuvring, one gathers from Froissart that it usually consisted of an attempt to gain the most favourable position for giving battle, and that the battle itself was decided in a *coup de main*, or fierce hand-to-hand fight. This settled, victors and vanquished alike needed a fortified place where they could rest and recuperate, and so be ready to fight another day.

The next illustrations (*101, 102*) are of a fourteenth-century castle, and have been made from Bodiam, in Sussex. All readers who go for summer holidays to the south coast should, if they have not already done so, pay a visit to this wonderful ruin. Licence to build the castle was granted to Sir Edward Dalyngrage in 1386; so the building dates from the end of the fourteenth century. The builder of Bodiam fought at Crécy and Poitiers, and the castle was probably built out of his share of the spoils. The victors in those days held the vanquished to ransom, and, as Froissart explains, very considerable sums had to be paid by the captives before they were allowed to go home.

Now for a consideration of the plan and sketch. Bodiam stands four-square in the centre of a moat fed by a stream. It is very French in character, and may have owed some of its inspiration to castles seen by its builder when on active service. Here is a point that we should bear in mind: the Crusades and the French Wars did a great deal to help the peaceful arts; for English soldiers returned home with memories of all that they had seen abroad, and put these new ideas into practice in their native country.

This fourteenth-century castle was entered by a timbered causeway across the moat, 1 on plan, defended by fortified bridge-heads at the moat side and before the barbican, at 2; while sections of the causeway have been made to act like a drawbridge, as an additional precaution. The causeway has long since disappeared; it should be noticed that the main approach was contrived with a sharp turn to the right at the point of entry, which prevented any sudden rush of men forcing a passage by sheer weight; also that the attackers on the causeway were under fire from the castle walls.

The barbican at 4 had a drawbridge at 3, which, with the portcullis, was worked from a room over the gateway, itself closed with strong oak doors. The turrets at the side of the barbican, besides being battlemented, are provided with the corbelling forward called machicolation, of which we saw the beginnings in the thirteenth-century castle. Here at Bodiam it has been developed in a very beautiful way; and the garrison could pour down boiling liquids on to the heads of the besiegers through holes in the floor without exposing themselves. From the battlemented top of the barbican and its loop-holed walls the garrison could also keep up a galling fire on the causeway and its approaches.

There was another drawbridge at 5, before the gatehouse proper at 6, which was defended in much the same way as the barbican; but here there were three portcullises, and cunning staircases contrived with very narrow and easily defended doors; so that, if the first compartment of the main entrance were lost, the besieged could retreat upstairs and pour down liquids, and shoot at the besiegers through holes in the vault called meurtrièrs. Even if the inner courtyard were forced, the besiegers could be shot at from all parts, and would find themselves, as in a thirteenth-century castle, not wholly masters of the situation. The outer walls are flanked by towers on all sides, so that the defenders could fire along the face of the wall at scaling parties.

The barracks for the garrison were at 7, and the chapel with small room for the priest at 8. The house part of the castle was on the side immediately opposite the entrance. The hall, which remains the principal apartment of castle, as of manor-house, was at 9, with the lord's private rooms at 10. Butteries and pantries were at 11, and the kitchen at 12, and there appears to have been an entrance, probably for the lord's use, at 13, approached by another causeway across the moat. At 14 was what may have been a kitchen and dining-hall for the garrison.

The reader will observe how closely the plan of the castle resembles the house of the period. We find the entrance to the hall immediately opposite the gatehouse, leading into the screens; and the relation of the buttery, pantry, and kitchen

101 A Castle of the time of Richard II, based on Bodiam, Sussex
("Decorated" style)

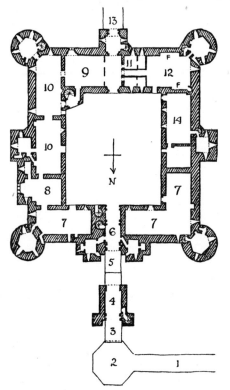

102 Plan of the Castle

1 Causeway across
2 Barbican
3 Drawbridge
4 Barbican
5 Drawbridge
6 Gatehouse
7 Barracks
8 Chapel
9 Hall
10 Private Rooms
11 Butteries and pantries
12 Kitchen
13 Private entrance
14 A kitchen and dining-hall

on one side, and the lord's rooms and solar on the other, is much the same as in the thirteenth-century house shown in fig. *68*, and the fourteenth-century one in this chapter(*103*). What Sir Edward did was to take the English plan and put high walls and flanking towers all round, and so keep, in a much strongly fortified building, the arrangement of rooms to which he was accustomed. The rooms on the first floor are reached by the circular staircases in the towers.

If we go to Bodiam, we must not think of it as a pretty ruin, or spend most of our time admiring the water-lilies and the little moor-hens pattering to and fro. The castle was built by a very tough old fighting man for the definite purpose of withstanding siege, and to this end it is most admirably adapted. Forgetting lilies and red-legged moor-hens, we must think of the castle as it was at the end of the fourteenth century, all brand-new and sparkling white, re-people it with lords and ladies and men-at-arms, and let it be the frame to a picture of the period. Froissart's *Chronicles* will help us to supply the atmosphere. He was in attendance on the Black Prince in 1366; and his book gives us an unforgettable account of that soldier's good and bad deeds. Wherever it is possible, we should study the records of contemporary writers—Jocelin of Brakelond, William of Malmesbury, Froissart, Chaucer, and all the others down to Pepys and Evelyn, describe their own period far more vividly than the historians of a later age.

COAL-MINING

But, from warfare and castle-planning, we must return to everyday things. We are so accustomed to-day to using coal, that we may not remember that, although coal was known and worked, it was not in everyday use in the house. The Romans worked it in England, but in outcrops only, and a great deal of the early coal was quarried from the cliffs by the sea-shore and washed up by the sea. It was thought to be a mineral, and in 1300 was called "burning stone". It was used chiefly in furnaces to burn lime; but, owing to the lack of chimneys, the fumes that it gave off made it too unpleasant for household use.

By the end of the fourteenth century, pits were being dug, chiefly in the North, for coal, and water was being drained out by means of subterranean drains, running from the pits in high ground downhill to some river level. Not until the end of the sixteenth century were pumps used for drainage.

One great bar to wide coal-distribution was the difficulty of cartage; and unless the mines were near the sea or a river, so that it could be readily shipped and so carried to its destination, its weight prevented its transport in large quantities by land. As it came by water from Newcastle, it was for long known in London as "sea-cole".

In 1554, a Venetian writing of England says: "In the North towards Scotland they find a certain sort of earth almost mineral which burns like charcoal and is extensively used by blacksmiths, and but for the bad odour which it leaves, it would be yet more employed as it gives great heat and costs but little." Not until the reign of Charles II, when fireplaces became smaller, chimneys more efficient and transport easier, did coal begin to take its place in the household.

THE HOUSE

Figs. *89, 103–4*, are of a fourteenth-century house built about 1341—a considerable improvement on that of the thirteenth century(*68*). The hall is no longer on the first floor, but is now on the ground floor; it is altogether a much more habitable place; the windows come right down, so that you can look out into the courtyard; and inside it is brighter and much more cheerful—less like a prison than it used to be. The hall, in its new arrangement, is more than ever the most important room in the house, and the centre of all the life of the place. The solar, or withdrawing-room, still remains on the first floor, over the cellar, just as it was in the century before; and here the lord retired when he wanted to be by himself, see his friends quietly, or go to bed. The wardrobe remained here, where the clothes were made and kept, and there were washing and lavatory arrangements for the private use of the family.

Both the hall and solar have separate roofs of their own, and look as if they had been placed side by side after being built, instead of being joined up under one roof as they were in the next century. The same idea is reflected in Henry III's instructions to the keepers of his houses, when he orders them to build a hall, a kitchen, or a chamber rather than a complete house. The hall in our illustration goes right up to the roof, and so has

159

103 A House of the time of Edward III, based on Penshurst Place, Kent
("Decorated" style)

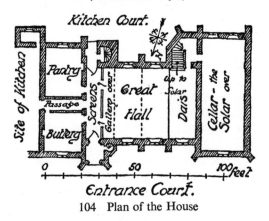

104 Plan of the House

the effect of cutting off all communication between the solar and the first-floor rooms on the other side of the house. The kitchen and offices have been improved by the addition of a buttery and pantry between the hall and kitchen(*104*). There is a staircase in the entrance porch, leading to a room above, and on to the minstrels' gallery, over the screens, looking down into the hall;

160

and these stairs led up to the battlements over the porch, and terminated in an octagonal turret with a fighting-top shown in the drawing.

Another addition in this century was a room provided on the first floor over the pantry and buttery, which corresponded to the solar on the other side. In the sketch it is shown as having the same kind of window, and this room was probably used as a spare bedroom would be nowadays, to house important guests. In the fifteenth century we shall see how all these arrangements remained, with still further improvements.

A little boy, to whom this drawing was shown, remarked that it was a "funny house—just like a church"; and this is quite true; and he might have added that all buildings were then more or less alike in detail, but varied in plan to suit the purpose for which they were intended. There was only one style of architecture; and the windows of the house show why we now call it "Decorated": they have begun to be filled with patterned tracery, which has a richer effect than the plain narrow windows of the thirteenth century, or "Early English" period.

So far as the surroundings of the house are concerned, there would have been an entrance courtyard in front, surrounded by stables, barracks, and so forth, and having a gatehouse on the side opposite the entrance porch of the house. At the back would be a kitchen court, with additional offices such as bakery and brewhouse; and the whole would be surrounded by a wall, or moat, depending on the character of the country. But, although the building is still defended, we see that, as conditions grew more settled, people were becoming more and more interested in the idea of comfort.

The figures in the foreground show a hunting party of the period. Hunting was to remain for a long time the chief amusement of the lord, when he was not engaged in statecraft or fighting.

The illustration(89) is of the hall interior, and shows the dais end. This was raised one step; and here was placed the high table, the seat behind which often had a high back, decorated with carved and moulded tracery, and standing against a piece of tapestry on the wall. The other tables were placed at the sides of the hall. At the left-hand side of the dais is shown an arched opening over the stairs leading up to the solar on the first floor; the small door at the side led to the

161

105 A Fourteenth-Century Hall ("Decorated" Style)

cellar. The little window over the high table looked out into the hall from the solar, perhaps so that the lord could pop his head out if the retainers made too much noise after he had gone to bed. The cellar, under the solar, was constructed at the back of the wall behind the high table. The fireplace of the hall was often in the middle of the floor; and the smoke had to find its way up and out of a louvre in the roof above. There was a slightly raised hearth, on which the iron fire-dogs stood, and logs were stacked up against them: one advantage must have been that

106 The Vir- you could make a complete circle round the fire,
gin of the and another that no heat was lost. So we must
Annunciation. think of the retainers, sitting all around on a
A Carved Oak winter's night, cracking nuts and jokes, and telling
Figure from hunting tales or old romances. The hall win-
Wells dows, coming nearly down to the ground, show

that sunlight and fresh air were beginning to be valued.

The roof is an interesting development of that shown in our illustration of a thirteenth-century solar. Instead of the tie-beams going across the hall, the roof is tied together by the collar-beams at a higher level. The roof at Penshurst, on which we have based our drawing, is a very fine piece of

107   Lower Brockhampton, Herefordshire.
From a drawing by Sydney R. Jones

163

carpenters' work, with a span of nearly 39 feet. The use of figures as corbels for the roof principals is interesting. The carvers often did very beautiful work. Fig. *106* shows a figure, carved in oak and painted, from the Hall of the Vicars Choral, Wells. At the close of the century, 1394, in Richard II's reign, the wonderful open-timbered roof over Westminster Hall was constructed, with a span of about 68 feet. It still exists, and is considered the finest example of a Gothic timbered roof. This type, known as the "hammer-beam", became general in the fifteenth century.

108   Detail of the Table Trestles at Penshurst

In the West Country particularly there was also a strong tradition of timber building. We show the interesting little group of buildings at Lower Brockhampton, hidden away near Bromyard in Herefordshire(*107*). The house dates from about the end of the fourteenth century; and the timber framing shows on the inside. The roof and stair remind us of Stokesay. The little gatehouse is of the fifteenth century; but the style is unchanged. There is a moat and a ruined chapel.

While we are on the subject of carpentry, we should like to draw attention to the tables shown in fig. *89*. These are of the "trestle type", the actual table-top being made of boards clamped together and supported on trestles. The top could be lifted off and stood against the wall, and the trestles put away in a corner. The tables at Penshurst are 27 feet long by 3 feet wide, and made of oak. Fig. *108* gives a detail of one of the trestles.

BARNS AND TIMBER-BUILDING

On page 40 we suggested that the Anglo-Saxon house was rather like a glorified barn. Fig. *109* shows the roof detail of a beautiful Tithe Barn at Peterborough, which was built in 1307. It was 144 feet long by 32 feet wide; the roof was all framed up in oak, and the walls were of stone. It sounds incredible; but this barn happened to stand on three "desirable" plots of land, which lent themselves to "development" and, when the plots were sold for £1,100, the old barn was thrown in, and pulled down. More recently the equally fine great barn of Great Barton, Suffolk, was also destroyed. Its construction was very similar to the Peterborough example; but the timbers were rougher and less shaped.

There is something peculiarly Anglo-Saxon, or Northern, in this timber-building tradition, and it continued to exist side by side with the houses built in brick or stone. Fig. *110* shows

109   The Roof Detail of a Tithe Barn at Peterborough,
destroyed in 1899

110   The Hall at Tiptofts, near Saffron Walden, Essex
(The later additions removed)

a fourteenth-century house, all framed up in oak, like a barn.
The drawing shows the interior of the Hall of Tiptofts Manor
House, at Wimbish, near Saffron Walden, in Essex, as it would
have appeared when it was built about 1330. Tiptofts is now a
farm-house, and many alterations and additions have considerably altered its appearance. But it is still possible to trace
the original plan. We ourselves have climbed up into the roof,
from one of the bedrooms added later, and picked off soot
which had been deposited on the rafters, in earlier times, when

166

111   Costume of the "Perpendicular" Period. Fifteenth Century

the Hall was warmed by a central fire. The plan on fig. *110* shows how closely Tiptofts resembled Penshurst.

In the Hall, the posts which support the roof are morticed on the sides next the walls to take rails, as shown in our drawing; and it looks as if these may have been used to make recesses for beds at night.

VAULTING AND SCULPTURE

We can now trace the development of vaulting in the fourteenth century. The design of that shown in fig. *118* is very interesting. The kitchen is octagonal, and the builders wished to leave a central space through which the steam could escape. This was the problem that they confronted; and, though the vault looks complicated, the solution they found simple. The dotted lines on the plan at the top right hand show the lines of the vaulting ribs over; and, if these are studied, it will be seen that the vault is constructed with eight semicircular arches, which cross from side to side, and that their intersection at the top provides the opening for the octagonal lantern. This drawing may be compared with the others in the vaulting series, and is of interest because it shows how adaptable vaulting was as a roofing system. Then, of course, there are all the beautiful chapter-houses with a central shaft. These, however, we must leave for the moment, and concentrate on the more ordinary type.

Fig. *112* is of a fourteenth-century lierne vault, so called because of the short ribs that have been added between the longer ones at the top of the vault. Lierne comes from the French verb *lier*, to bind; and these small ribs do, in fact, bind, and join up, the vault at its flattest and weakest point. If the reader turns back to the drawing of a thirteenth-century vault(*66*) he will see that there has been little alteration in the general construction, the aisle roof can still be compared to a pointed tunnel, crossed at right angles by other tunnels of the same shape. So the developments in fourteenth-century vaulting are an improvement rather than an alteration in type. We still have the groin ribs going diagonally across each bay, and the transverse ones going across the aisle, with wall ribs against the outer walls; but a ridge rib has been added at the apex or crown of the vault; and there are now intermediate ribs between the

112 A "Decorated" Vault

groins and the transverse ribs, and the groins and the wall ribs, and these are called tiercerons. They served to reduce the space and make the construction of the web between the ribs easier. At the intersection of the ribs, carved bosses were formed, which were often carved either with foliage or with groups of

170

113   Carved Crockets, Selby Abbey, Yorkshire

figures. At Norwich Cathedral the three hundred and twenty-eight bosses in the nave vault, added by Bishop Lyhart, are very beautiful. They begin in the easternmost bay, with sculptured representations of the Creation, and so progress, bay by bay, with all the incidents of Bible history; there is the Last Supper, Noah builds his Ark on one; the Tower of Babel is shown as a medieval fortress on another. Joseph is stripped of his coat of many colours; and Samson rends the lion, as in fig. *113* on crockets from Selby Abbey Church. The Childhood of our Lord is shown; His Life and Death; and in the end bay one boss shows the Last Judgment. The Devil has tied up all the wicked in neat bundles, rather like asparagus, and with a pitchfork is thrusting the bundles, one by one, down into the bottomless pit.

Think of all this work, spent in carving pieces of stone not more than a foot or so across! Of all the thousands of people who enter Norwich Cathedral, probably very few know of this treasure in the vault, seventy-two feet above their heads. A good glass is necessary to pick out the beautiful detail; and some might consider that the sculptor's labour of love had been thrown away. But the medieval artist thought quite differently. He was engaged in beautifying God's House, and determined that it should be as beautiful and as perfect as it could be made by human hands; he did not count the labour, or the cost, or the time, or the trouble. This nave vault is an indication of its builders' character—they were both good men and fine craftsmen. All the bosses they produced, with another wonderful series in the cloister, have recently been carefully cleaned and picked out in colour.

Here our readers may perhaps object that our illustration is of a fourteenth-century vault, while Norwich is fifteenth. The answer is, that the Gothic periods dovetail one into another. Lierne ribs were introduced as early as 1230 in Lincoln Chapterhouse, and continued right up to the days of fan vaulting; and we find the latter as early as 1412 in the Gloucester Cloister. It is less important to remember dates and names of styles than to discover the basic secrets of construction.

The fourteenth-century builders used the lierne rib quite as much for decorative as for practical purposes, and with it formed pleasant patterns along the crowns of their vaults. At length, the effect became so complicated, with so many ribs joining, separating and rejoining in such a diversity of maze-like patterns, that they could make no further progress. The next development will be described in our chapter on the fifteenth century.

MEALS AND TABLE-MANNERS

Fig. *89* shows a banquet being held at the high table, drawn from a brass at King's Lynn, which commemorates a "Peacock Feast" given to Edward III. The retainers bring the dishes, and hand them to the squires at the sides of the table; for squires were expected to be able to carve properly and to serve their lord and lady. The squires were former pages; and such attendance was regarded as a step in their knightly education. We learn that kings' sons were taught to carve before their father at table.

The following is an extract from Hugh Russell's *Boke of Nurture*, telling a page of his various duties, and how to perform them.

> Put the salt on the right hand of your lord; on its left a trencher or two. On their left a knife, then white rolls, and beside, a spoon folded in a napkin. Cover all up. At the other end set a salt and two trenchers; cut your loaves equal, take a towel 2½ yards long by its ends, fold up a handful from each end, and in

the middle of the folds lay eight loaves or buns, bottom to bottom; put a wrapper on the top, twist the ends of the towel together, smooth your wrapper, and open the end of it before your lord.

The boys are also instructed to serve their lord on bended knee, to bow when answering him, and not to sit until told to do so. Grace was said before and after meals, and before a feast, heralded by a trumpet, servants, or pages, entered with basins, ewers, and napkins, and the guests washed their hands. The host and chief guests dined at the "high table", which was generally raised on a dais, while other tables, placed down the sides of the hall, accommodated those of lesser importance. Tables were covered with a cloth; and the platters were wooden or pewter, and in great houses of gold or silver.

Until the middle of the fourteenth century only knives and spoons appear to have been in use; and there were not many of them. Most people still ate with their fingers, and everyone threw the bones and scraps on to the rushes strewn on the floor, where the dogs scrambled and fought over the titbits.

But dainty feeding was considered an accomplishment, as we can see in Chaucer's description of a Prioresse:

> At meté wel y-taught was she with-alle,
> She leet no morsel from hir lippés falle,
> Ne wette hir fyngrés in hir saucé depe.
> Wel koude she carie a morsel and wel kepe,
> Thát no drope ne fille upon hire breste;
> In curteisie was set ful muchel hir leste.
> Hire over-lippé wyped she so clene,
> That in hir coppe ther was no ferthyng sene
> Of grecé, whan she dronken hadde hir draughte.

But the Prioresse must have been the exception, or Chaucer would scarcely have mentioned the fact that she did not dip her fingers deep in the sauce.

A fourteenth-century banquet would have included many curious contrasts—the pomp and ceremony attending these feasts, the beautiful plate on the tables, the wonderful tapestry on the walls, and the rushes on the floor, made foul by the débris thrown down by the feasters and scrambled and fought for by the dogs of the house.

Although spoons and knives were used, we hear very little of forks, except that in Edward II's reign we are told that

Piers Gaveston had, among other treasures, some silver forks, "for eating pears". We also learn that John, Duke of Brittany, used a fork of silver with which to pick up "soppys".

Men when hunting and riding carried knives stuck through their wallets; and these they often used at meals. A picture of such a wallet can be seen on page 201. Both knives and spoons, like almost everything else in this period, were generally of beautiful design and workmanship.

One platter was laid for every two persons; and a knight and his partner ate off the same plate and used one drinking vessel between them; and indeed, in poorer houses, one cup did

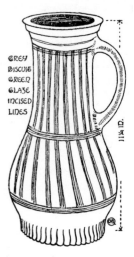

GREY
BISCUIS
GREEN
GLAZE
INCISED
LINES

11¾ ID.

114   Peasant Pottery

service for the entire family. Drinking vessels were very seldom of glass, but were usually fashioned of metal, horn, or wood.

But to revert to our table as laid for a feast. The chief ornament was the great salt-cellar. This was large, of costly material and beautifully wrought, and was placed in front of the chief personage, who alone used it, smaller salt-cellars being placed before the other guests.

The "nef", a jewelled model of a ship, which contained spice to add flavour to the various dishes, was also borne to the table and placed thereon with much ceremony. Our forbears liked their food very much flavoured and spiced. Accompanying the "nef" was the "wassail" bowl, in which to drink toasts. This was called the "mazer", because "mazer" is the old term for maple, and it was of this wood that the bowl was carved.

115   A Bronze Ewer found near York
(*British Museum*)

116   A Housewife with a Chest and Lantern

"Mazer" bowls usually had covers, and were ornamented with precious metals.

We noted, when writing of the thirteenth century, that the potters of the Middle Ages did not produce anything that could be compared with the works of classical antiquity. The same remains true of the fourteenth century. Fig. *114* is just a pleasant piece of peasant pottery. In the finer houses they probably used metal instead(*115*). Figs. *116* and *117* show some of the household gear used for storing goods or holding wine and water.

Dinner was served between nine and ten in the morning, and the next meal was supper, at five o'clock. There is an old French tag that runs as follows:

Lever à cinq, diner à neuf,
Souper à cinq, coucher à neuf,
Fait vivre d'ans nonante et neuf.

The supper-table was lighted with torches or with candles made of wax. Minstrels were always in attendance, and reading aloud was a favourite form of entertainment. In noblemen's houses there was always a fool or jester; and during the mealtime he would enliven the company with his jests and capers; or the minstrels would

117   A Cask, Tub and Water-pots

175

recite histories of noble deeds and amusing anecdotes, or they would play on various musical instruments, the chief performer usually employing the bagpipe.

It is odd to reflect that, after all this display of beautiful plate and ornament, and after the feasting and ceremony, lit by candles that shone on the brocades and jewels of the guests, as soon as night came and the tables had been taken down, the hall would be filled with a motley collection of retainers, who slept huddled together among the rushes on the floor round the great fire in the middle.

Chaucer, in his "Tale of Sir Thopas", tells of a knight taking food before setting out on adventure. He speaks of the minstrels and jesters, and of the mazer or loving-cup:

> "Do come," he seyde, "my mynstrales,
>   And geestours for to tellen tales,
>   Anon in myn armýnge;
>   Of rómances that been roiales [royal],
>   Of Popés and of Cardinales,
>   And eek [also] of love-likýnge

> "They fette hym first, the sweeté wyn [wine]
>   And mede eek in a mazelyn,
>   And roial spicerye;
>   And gyngébreed that was ful fyn,
>   And lycorys, and eek comyn [cummin],
>   With sugre that is so trye [choice]."

KITCHENS AND COOKING

After so much talk about food, it is only right that our next illustration (*118*) should be of a kitchen, such as was built for a king's palace, a noble's house, or a monastery. Its dimensions—36 feet across the widest part—were by no means unusual at this period. The early house, as we have already explained, was often more like a series of buildings placed side by side than a block all under one roof. The kitchen had often been built, for greater protection against fire, as a separate building, connected with the hall by a covered way; and, even when it had become more closely joined up with the main building, it was often only of one storey in height, with what is called a lantern over, from which the steam and smell of cooking

176

118   A Kitchen in the time of Edward III ("Decorated" style)

could readily escape. The passage then, shown in the middle
of the picture, would lead into the hall, through the screens,
having the buttery on one side, where the wine was kept under
the charge of the butler (from *boutelle*, a bottle), and the pantry
on the other, where the bread, salt, cups, and platters were
kept.

So far as the kitchen itself is concerned, we must imagine a much busier scene than any preparations we have known in our own houses. In *Uncle Tom's Cabin* there is an amusing description of the interior of a kitchen in the Southern States, presided over by a cheerful old negress who evolved wonderful dinners out of chaos. Meanwhile, all the rest of the establishment came in and assisted, contributing to the clatter. Periodically, there was a general clear-up. The medieval kitchen must have been rather like this—without the clearing-up. The impression left in one's mind is that the hall formed the centre of village life, and that, if you belonged to the land, you took your part quite naturally in what was going on at the hall. So we must imagine a good deal of noise and confusion and running about: a deal of dirt, one is afraid, but much cheerfulness.

The kitchen was provided with two, or more, open fireplaces, as shown, the one on the left hand being used for making stews, broths, or boiling meat. It must be remembered that in the fourteenth century there were no swedes, or other roots, for feeding cattle in the winter; so the beasts were largely killed off and salted down; and their meat, of course, had to be boiled. This was one of the reasons for preserving game, which provided the lord with fresh meat in the winter. Joints and poultry were roasted before an open fire, on a spit resting in two grooved stumps, and turned by a boy. Food prepared in this way was often served on the spit. On the other side of the kitchen, as shown by the plan at the top left-hand side of the picture, were ovens where the baking was done. The oven played a great part in fourteenth-century cooking. Generally shaped in the form of a large oval, it was built in the thickness of the wall with an arched roof over it. When it was to be used, a bundle of faggots was placed inside and lighted, and an iron door closed in front. Once the faggots had burned out, and made the air in the oven and all the brickwork round it very hot, the door was opened, and the ashes raked aside; then in went the bread and cakes, the pies and pasties, the door was closed, and, when the oven cooled down, the cooking was done. Very primitive ovens may have been used in connection with the open fires where logs were burnt and the ashes allowed to accumulate. To this day, in the

West Country, some of the older people do their cooking in this manner; the ashes in the open wood-fire are cleared away, and the joint or pie put on the hearth, and covered with a rough iron cover, and this again is covered with the hot ashes. Old country people, who are used to it, prefer food that has been thus cooked; and, as such customs have been handed down for generations, it may well be one of the methods that the fourteenth-century cooks used.

In Wright's *Homes of Other Days* the following list of medieval kitchen utensils is given:

> A brandreth, or iron tripod, for supporting the caldron over the fire; a caldron, a dressing-board and dressing-knife, a brass pot, a posnet, or saucepan, a frying-pan, a gridiron, a spit, a gobard, a mier for making bread-crumbs, a flesh-hook, a scummer, a ladle, a pot-stick, a slice for turning meat in the frying-pan, a pot-hook, a mortar and pestle, a pepper-quern, a platter, a saucer for making sauce.

From Turner's *Domestic Architecture* we learn the contents of the larder at Fynchate, in the year 1311: "the carcases of twenty oxen, and fifteen pigs, of herrings eight thousand, of dograves (a sea fish) seven score, twenty pounds of almonds, thirty of rice, six barrels of lard, enough oatmeal to last till Easter, two quarters of salt."

Chaucer talks of mortrewès, and an old recipe for this dish directs that hens and pork be employed, and "hewe it small, and grounde it alle to doust"; it was then to be mixed with bread-crumbs, yolks of eggs, and pepper, and then boiled with ginger, sugar, salt, and saffron. Herring-pie was another dish we should regard as unusual; lampreys are historical; and spices were used in abundance. Our fourteenth-century men had got good tough palates—Chaucer's Frankelen liked sauces "poinant and sharpe". Honey was in constant use for making mead and sweetening; and cider and beer were generally drunk. But we can never understand how the medieval housekeeper got on without potatoes.

119 Sawing Wood

FAIRS AND MARKETS

Markets, where all things not grown or made by the goodman and his wife could be bought, and their surplus produce sold in return, were a great feature of medieval life. Country people had to pay a tax either to the king or to the landowner as rent for stalls or for leave to stand and sell their goods in the market. An old English word for buying is "cheaping"; the merchant was the cheapman or chapman; and one street where stalls were set up in London is still known as Cheapside and another as Eastcheap. There is also Chipping Hill near Witham in Essex, and many market towns like Campden, Sodbury, and Barnet have, or had, the prefix "Chipping".

The taxes and dues payable to the king were all accounted at the courts of the exchequer; so-called after the great chequered table at which all accounts were calculated in the medieval manner with squares and counters.

In the twelfth and thirteenth centuries markets were often

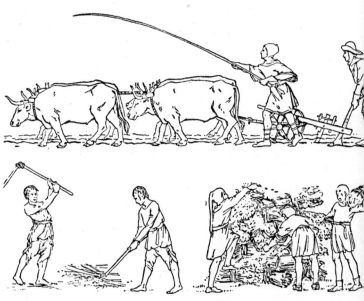

120 Agriculture at the time of Edward I

held in the local churchyard; but in 1285 a statute was passed forbidding this practice, and it was discontinued. Markets were held weekly, mainly for local produce and for articles of everyday use; but once or twice a year great fairs were held to which merchants from overseas brought their goods and silks, spices, jewels and linens. The rules governing the markets were strict; and a hut called the "Tolbooth" was set apart to accommodate a court dealing with all discussions and difficulties, with power to punish offenders. This tolbooth later became a permanent building in the Town Hall of each place; and the court held therein was known as the "piepowder" court or court of the wayfarers, the "pieds poudrés". The word "Tolbooth" is still in active use in Scotland, where it designates a combined town hall and prison. At the great fairs some of the large gilds or companies were given various privileges and, in return, were obliged to organise and police them; and, to judge by what one reads of a thirteenth- or fourteenth-century crowd, this must have been an arduous undertaking.

om the Luttrell Psalter

181

LIFE ON THE FARM

121   Bob Apple

We must now move away into the country to find out how in the fourteenth-century people passed their time there.

One of the most wonderful manuscripts of the world is the *Luttrell Psalter* (now the property of the British nation), which is supposed to have been produced between 1320 and 1340, for Sir Geoffrey Luttrell of Irnham, Lincolnshire, who died in 1345. It is full of admirable little drawings of horses and carts, peasants and windmills; and the artist, in the most obliging way, seems to have tried to give us an exact idea of everyday life and things in England just before the Black Death. From this point of view, the value of the Psalter is enormous; for that terrible plague brought about great changes in the conditions of English life.

We have seen how in the thirteenth century the conditions of agriculture remained much the same as in the twelfth, and that the villein was winning his freedom. This continued until the Black Death. Cultivation was very simple, carried on according to what is known as the three-field system: the arable land in the village was divided up into three big fields, and planted in rotation— one with wheat, another with barley or oats, while the third remained fallow. Rye was grown as well as peas, beans, and vetches. The land was turned over by oxen yoked to wooden ploughs (*120*). Fig. *28* illustrates the wheeled plough that appears in the Bayeux Tapestry. In the *Luttrell Psalter* a "swing" plough is being used; and this type has lasted

122   A Wayfarer

182

down to our own times. Fig. *123* depicts a wooden plough that we sketched at Marsworth, in Bedfordshire. Very little manuring was done, except by folding sheep over the land. It will be remembered how in the twelfth century there were quarrels between the convent and townsfolk of Bury St. Edmunds, who were supposed to turn their sheep into the abbey fields, and demurred at so doing. Next to the plough in the illustration (*120*) a couple are apparently breaking up the larger clods with wooden mallets. Then comes harrowing, and the illustration shows that fourteenth-century harrows were much like ours. The boy has a job after his own heart, slinging stones at birds. Sowing follows; and this of course was done broadcast by hand. The next couple are weeding with rather curiously shaped implements, succeeded by reapers who use a hand sickle, the corn being cut high in the stalk. Stacking and threshing with hand flails are the last two operations represented.

One great point about the Psalter drawings is the care bestowed on all the practical details: how harness was fitted on, the way carts were made. And this leads one to suppose that the drawings were studies from life, not merely pictures derived from the artist's imagination. If this is so, it is obvious that before the Black Death the peasant was well and warmly clothed. Farm-labourers of to-day would be glad to have the gauntleted gloves some of the Psalter figures are wearing. Generally they wear the usual dress of their class, a tunic and chausses, with the typical chaperon, or hood, for head covering; the men using the flail wear long breeches-like chausses, but without feet, and so arranged that they can be pulled up high

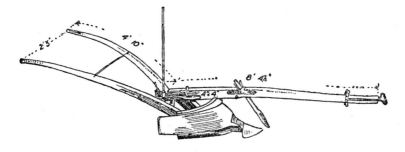

123   A Plough, from Marsworth

as shown, and fastened to the belt, leaving the legs free. The man weeding is wearing wooden clogs. But, no doubt, conditions differed enormously, and many of the country labouring folk were miserably clothed, fed, and housed. Their wretched state and rough ragged clothing is described in the pathetic lines on the Ploughman in *Piers Plowman's Crede*, about 1394. It is probably accurate, if highly coloured, and accords with the graphic picture of the poor cottar's interior in the *Four States of Society* by Jean Bonchardon at Amiens, illustrated in Bouchot's *Exposition des Primitifs français*.

124   A Tinker

> And as I went by the way . weeping for sorrow
> I saw a poor man by me . on the plough hanging
> His coat was of a clout . that cary (coarse cloth) was called
> His hood was full of holes . and his hair cut
> With his nobby shoes . patched full thick
> His tongue peeped out . as he the earth trod
> His hosen overhung his gaiter . on every side
> All beslobbered in mire . as he the plough followed
> Two mittens so scanty . made all of patches
> The fingers were worn . and full of mud hung
> This fellow wallowed in the muck . almost to the ankle
> Four heifers before him . that weak had become
> You could count all their ribs . so wretched they were
> His wife walked by him . with a long goad
> In a coat cut short . cut full high
> Wrapped in a winnowing sheet . to cover her from the weather
> Barefoot on the bare ice . that the blood followed
> And at the field end lay . a little bowl
> And on it lay a little child . wrapped in rags
> And two of two years old . on another side
> And all they sang a song . that was sad to hear
> They all cried a cry . a note full of care
> The poor man sighed sore and said . "Children be still."

The effects of the Black Death, in 1348, reduced the number of labourers by about one-half; whole families died out and

125   An Assault on a Castle by a movable scaling-tower, with defenders
        hurling stones from a trebuchet. Note early cannon

A reconstruction by G. Kruger Gray

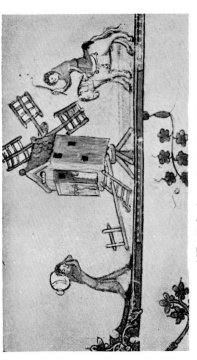

126 Women snaring birds with decoys

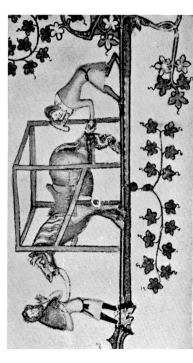

127 Bringing grist to the mill

128 A cart with cask—not so different from the Bayeux Tapestry

129 Horse-shoeing in a frame—found also 300 years later

130   The Tethered Hen.
From the Luttrell Psalter

their holdings reverted to the lords; the Court rolls, which formed a record of all the proceedings of the manor, often come to an abrupt end, with a gap, before they start again, which tells a tale of death and suffering. When the plague was over, the lords had more land on their hands than they knew what to do with; and the few remaining labourers began to demand higher wages.

We have described how, in the thirteenth century, the villein had often purchased his freedom from his lord by payment of a fine, and how this custom had developed because it suited the conditions of the period. But it was a custom rather than a law. The latter part of the extract overleaf from William Langland, the poet of the period, shows that by 1394 the field labourer found himself in a position to demand high wages and appetising food, and could indulge in a thorough-paced grumble if conditions were not exactly to his liking.

It must have seemed like base ingratitude to the landowners of the day when the labourers, who had gained their freedom in prosperous times by very small payments, now that bad times had come wanted to profit by the straits in which the community found itself. The result was the passing of the Statute of Labourers in 1349, which sought to limit prices and the wages of labourers and, later on, to bind them to the land again. This, combined with taxation to finance the French War, led to the Peasants' Rebellion at the end of the century. Sheep-farming received a great impetus, because it required fewer men than the cultivation of arable land. Even more interesting is the custom, which started about this time, of letting farms on what are called stock- and land-leases. While the extremists were passing laws trying to reduce the villeins to serfs, and the villeins were resisting as best they could, the moderate men apparently put their heads together and evolved a scheme. The problem was to get the men to work; so conditions were made more attractive. In effect, the lords said: "Very well, if you will not come and work the land for me on the old terms, I will stock it for you with cattle and implements, which you must agree to render up at the end of your term; and you shall pay a rent for it." Here we see the origins of the farming system of to-day. But the system of common fields, with grazing rights, also remained in force until the end of the eighteenth century, when the Enclosure Acts finally did away with it.

This quotation from Langland's *Piers the Plowman* shows the short commons to which the labouring country folk were frequently reduced, and how they had often to eke out scanty fare until the plenteous time of harvest, when they feasted gloriously:

"I have no penny" quoth Piers . "Pullets for to buy
Nor neither geese nor piglets . but two green* cheeses
A few curds and cream . and an oaten cake
And two loaves of beans and bran . to bake for my little ones
And besides I say by my soul . I have no salt bacon
Nor no little eggs, by Christ . collops for to make
But I have parsley and leeks . and many cabbages
And besides a cow and a calf . and a cart mare
To draw afield my dung . the while the drought lasteth
And by this livelihood we must live . till lammas time [August]
And by that I hope to have . harvest in my croft
And then may I prepare the dinner . as I dearly like

"All the poor people those . peascods fatten
Beans and baked apples . they brought in their laps
Shalots and chervils . and ripe cherries many
And proffered pears these present . to please with hunger
All hunger eat in haste . and asked after more
Then poor folk for fear . fed hunger eagerly
With great leeks and peas . to poison hunger me thought
By then it came near harvest . new corn came to market
Then were folk glad . and fed hunger with the best
With good ale as Glutton taught . and got hunger to sleep
And when wasters wouldn't work . but wander about
Nor no beggar eat bread . that beans within were
But two sorts of fine white . or else of clean wheat

* Green=fresh or new.

188

> Nor no halfpenny ale . in nowise drink
> But of the best and the brownest . that in town is to sell
> Labourers that have no land . to live on, only their hands
> Deigned not to dine each day . on herbs not fresh gathered
> Have no penny-ale given them . nor no piece of bacon
> But if it be fresh flesh or fish . fried or baked
> And that warm or hot . to avoid chilling their bellies."

Thus famine was usual in bad years; and there does not seem to have been any system of storing the surplus of a good year against the advent of a bad one.

DOCTORS AND APOTHECARIES

We have noted (p. 79 and fig. *31*) that the doctor in the twelfth century was his own chemist and druggist; but during the thirteenth and fourteenth centuries separate pharmacies were gradually coming into existence and huge cargoes of drugs and spices were imported from Venice. We read of opium, rhubarb, senna, sugar, camphor, cloves, pepper, ginger, mace, cinnamon, and nutmeg being brought over in great galleys guarded by archers, so precious was the freight. Apothecaries sold spices and scents and sweetmeats, as well as drugs. The gild of Pepperers included drugs in their stock, as did the Spicers' Company; and in the fifteenth century the Grocers, or sellers "en Gros"(*152*), received their charter and were given the office of weighing all drugs that came into the country.

Chaucer speaks of apothecaries:

> Full ready had he [the physician] his apothecaries
> To send his drugges and his lectuaries.

It was in the fourteenth century, moreover, that an Italian physician wrote a treatise on the teeth and their decay, and gave a prescription for tooth-powder. Efforts were made at hygiene; a statute was passed in the fourteenth century to prevent the pollution of ditches and rivers; and in the thirteenth century London's first conduit brought water from the river to a fountain in Eastcheap. But it was not until the sixteenth century that any real progress was effected, and certain primitive waterworks with pumps and conduits were laid down. Bathing(*82*) was probably infrequent, although some illustrations are to be found of bathrooms consisting of a curtained alcove with a tub in it. For washing clothes, a lye made from wood ashes was used as soap; but, if this was used on the body, it cannot have been agreeable.

THE WINDMILL

Our next illustration(*131*) is of a windmill, the first in the book. It is sad that, as our civilisation progresses, it should blot out so many beautiful things. The sailing-ship is going, and the windmill has nearly gone; yet the latter was one of the loveliest things of the countryside. Because in a few years they will all have vanished, we have taken especial trouble to draw a series of the different types. We referred to the windmill in the *Windmill Psalter*, page 135. This is of the same "Post" type as fig. *131*, except that the trestles that support the post rest on the ground, and have not yet been raised on piers. The piers doubtless improved the mill by lifting the sails up into the wind. The next step was to enclose the piers, and form a round-house under the mill, as fig. *170* in our fifteenth-century chapter. In the *Luttrell Psalter*, 1320–40, there is a good windmill, and several post-mills appear in *The Romance of Alexander* (Bodleian Library, Oxford)(*127*). Now for the principle on which a mill works—it is rather like that of a screw-driven steamer. In the latter, the blades of the screw are set at an angle, so that, as the screw is turned, it eats its way into the water in much the same way as a screw goes into wood. It is the resistance of the water against the screw that sends the steamer forward. In a windmill, the sails attached to the arms offer a resistance to the wind; and, in this early type, a wooden lattice-work was covered with sails, laced on as shown in the drawing, and so arranged, again in ship-like fashion, that they could be furled when not in use. The outer ends of the sails are all in the same plane, but the outside tips or the ends of sails next to the axle are deflected. The wind blowing against the sails turns them around, just as the little celluloid vanes, sold as toys, are turned when one holds them and runs along. The screw of a steamer would be turned round if a sufficiently strong jet of water were directed against it.

This type is called the post-mill, because it turns on one great

131   A Medieval Windmill

132   A Char.   *From the Luttrel Psalter*

central post, supported by trestles as shown. It remained in use for a long time, and our fifteenth-century chapter contains an illustration that shows the whole working of the mill.

TRAVEL

Travelling about the country was still a difficult business, and most people made their journeys on horseback. All Chaucer's pilgrims rode to Canterbury. Carriages of a sort were used for special or state occasions; fig. *132* depicts a carriage of the kind that used to be called a char. As all the occupants are ladies, it may be that women of the richer classes were accustomed to travel in this fashion, while the men accompanied them on horseback. The team of five horses would have been necessary to pull such a cumbersome vehicle over the rough roads of the period; and it must have been used by the Court, or some great personage, as the char itself is elaborately decorated. The sides are panelled, and the semicircular top is covered with charac-

teristic ornament. This top was probably made of painted canvas, stretched over wooden hoops. This little travelling party, with its gaily decorated char, and the brilliant clothes of the ladies and horsemen, would have made a bright spot of colour. Froissart often tells us, when describing the Black Prince's army in France, that it was a goodly sight; and it is difficult for us, accustomed as we are to clothes of black and dingy grey, to picture the effect produced by a large gathering of medieval people. We should like to try the effect of splashing the twentieth-century

133   Stilts   City stockbroker all over with a really bright

yellow, and painting his friend the merchant a good vermilion. Bankers could be parti-coloured, and experiments made to see if this produced an appearance of greater cheerfulness.

PARTIES AND RECREATIONS

Talking of colour and gaiety leads us to games. In the fourteenth century we hear of cards being played, and of a curious game called "Ragman's Roll". In this, a roll or parchment was used, on which various verses were written describing the characters of the players, each verse having a string and seal attached. These seals hung down from the rolled-up parchment, and each person drew one of the seals, and had to take on the character attached to that particular verse. Games of questions and answers and of forfeits were also played, and dancing was very common. Many dances took place out of doors, and dancing often followed a picnic.

Chaucer, in "The Franklin's Tale", tells us of a party of young girls amusing themselves after dinner in the garden. One of them is in trouble, and the others try to persuade her to play and dance with them and so forget her grief. Chaucer tells the tale thus:

Hire friends sawe that it was no disport
To romen by the see, but disconfort,
And shopen [determined] for to pleyen somwher elles.
They leden hire by ryveres [rivers] and by welles,
And eek in othere places delitables [delectables];
They dauncen, and they pleyen at ches and tables [backgammon].
So on a day right in the morwe [morning] tyde,
Unto a garden that was ther bisyde,
In which that they hadde maad hir ordinaunce [given their orders]
Of vitaille, and of oother purveiaunce [providence],
They goon and pleye hem al the longé day,
And this was on the sixté morwe of May.

. . . .

At after dyner gonné they to daunce,
And synge also, save Dorigen allone,
Which made alwey hir compleint and hir moone.

We do not know what song they sang; but there is an original fourteenth-century MS. in the British Museum of a carol "Angelus ad Virginem" which Chaucer mentions in "The Milleres Tale":

> On which he made a nightes melodye
> So swetely, that all the chambre rong,
> And Angelus ad Virginem he song.

Our next illustration (*134*) is of a game called "Hot Cockles". It is played thus: one player kneels blindfolded, holding her hands behind her, while the others strike her hand, and she tries to guess the striker's name. The chief object seems to have been to knock over the "he" with the force of the blow. Indeed, the majority of games, not only for children but even those played by ladies and their knights, would nowadays appear very rough and the jokes that accompanied them extremely boisterous. "Hot Cockles" is found in the same form as late as the early eighteenth century, when the writer who describes it tells us that he was knocked over by the strength of the blow he received.

An amusing little sidelight on the roughness of the times is

134 "Hot Cockles"

135   Boys playing at Riding at the Quintain

thrown by Chaucer in his "Murrye [merry] words of the Hoost [host] to the monk". He says of his wife:

> Whan I bete my knaves [servants]
> She bryngeth me forth the greté clobbéd staves
> And crieth "Slee the doggés everichoon [everyone],
> And brek hem, bothé bak [back] and every boon [bone]."

Truly, punishment in those days must have been no light thing.

DECORATION

The fourteenth-century MS.(*140*) shows the delicate filigree-like scrollwork of perhaps the finest period of illumination, with lightly drawn angel figures. The miniature is now more realistic and in greater relief; the priest sprinkles the shrouded corpse with holy water as it is committed to the grave. It comes from a Book of Hours produced about the end of the fourteenth century. The tailpiece of this chapter shows a typical piece of the fourteenth-century ornament.

136   "Decorated" Ornament

Dates	Kings and Queens of England and France.	Famous Men.	Great Events, Sea Fights, and Land Battles.	Principal Buildings (B., Benedictine; C., Cistercian).
1400	Henry IV. Charles VI.	Luca della Robbia, 1400-82		York Central Tower, 1400-23
1401			Persecution of the Lollards	Christchurch, Hants
1402		Joan of Arc, 1402-31	Glendower Rebellion Battles of Homildon Hill and Shrewsbury	Lady Chapel, 1400, C.
1403			Rebellion of the Percies	
1413	Henry V., m. Catherine of France			St. Nicholas, Lynn, 1413-18
1414			Lollard Rising	
1415			War with France Siege of Harfleur and Agincourt	
1416			Use of gunpowder and guns	
1417			Siege of Rouen	
1420		William Caxton, 1420-91	Treaty of Troyes	
1421			Battle of Beaujé	Gloucester South Porch, West Nave, and Front, 1421-37
1422	Henry VI., m. Margaret of Anjou Charles VII.			
1423			Treaty of Amiens	
1424			Battle of Verneuil	St. Mary Radcliffe, Bristol, 1425-50
1428			Siege of Orleans	
1431			Siege of Compiègne Capture of Joan of Arc	
1435		Andrea della Robbia, 1435-1525	Treaty of Arras	South Wingfield Manor, 1435-50
1440				Eton School and Tattershall Castle, Lincs
1443				All Souls' College, Oxford
1445			Truce with France	
1447		Botticelli, 1447-1510		Magdalen College, Oxford
1448				Queens' College, Cambridge
1450			Jack Cade's Rebellion	Gloucester Tower, B., 1450-57, and Lady Chapel, 1457-72
1452		Leonardo da Vinci, 1452-1519		
1453			English driven out of France, 1430-53 Turks capture Constantinople	
1455			Wars of the Roses, 1455-61 First battle of St. Albans	King's College Chapel, Cambridge, 1460-85
1460			Battle of Northampton Battle of Wakefield, 1460	
1461	Edward IV., m. Elizabeth Woodville Louis XI.	Warwick, King-Maker	Battle of Mortimer's Cross Second battle of St. Albans, 1461 Battle of Towton	
1464			Battles of Hedgeley Moor and Hexham, 1464	Durham Central Tower, B., 1464-90
1471		Albert Dürer, 1471-1528	Battles of Barnet and Tewkesbury	
1475		Michelangelo, 1475-1564		Sherborne Nave, 1475-1504
1476			Caxton printing at Westminster	
1477		Titian, 1477-1576		
1480		Sir Thomas More, 1480-1535	War with Scotland	Magdalen College School, Oxford
1481				Great Chalfield, Wilts, and St. George's Chapel, Windsor, 1481-1537
1483	Edward V.; and Richard III., m. Anne Neville Charles VIII.	Martin Luther, b. 1483	Murder of Princes in the Tower	
1485	Henry VII., m. Elizabeth of York		Battle of Bosworth	
1486			Discovery of Cape of Good Hope	
1487			Lambert Simnel's Rebellion Battle of Stoke	Winchester Lady Chapel, 1487-1500
1491			War with France	Ely, Alcock's Chapel, 1488
1492			Columbus discovers America, and Rebellion of Perkin Warbeck, 1492-99	
1497		Holbein, 1497-1543	Sebastian Cabot lands in North America	
1498	Louis XII.			
1499				Henry VII. Chapel, 1503

137   Chart of the "Perpendicular" Period of Design, from 1400 to 1499

138 A Knight of the time of Henry VI

Chapter IV

FIFTEENTH CENTURY

THE fifteenth century was a period of transition: the Middle Ages were coming to an end, and the foundations of modern society were being laid. The epoch of feudal chivalry was replaced by that of discovery and commerce. Again social conditions were disturbed; for the French Wars of the three Henrys, IV, V, and VI, had an exhausting and unsettling effect. Even worse was the effect of the Wars of the Roses, the terrible civil conflict which followed them; and it is with relief that, towards the end of the century, we find England reunited under the shrewd and firm rule of Henry VII.

Throughout the world it was a period of tremendous happenings. Joan of Arc finally drove the English from France in 1453. In the same year the Turks captured Constantinople, and the dispersal of scholars and the classical tradition that they

197

brought with them introduced the new learning and prepared the way for the Reformation. By 1476 Caxton was hard at work at his printing press in Westminster, employing an invention as constructive as the development of gunpowder was destructive. By the close of the century the Cape of Good Hope had been visited, Columbus had discovered America, and Sebastian Cabot had landed on the transatlantic mainland.

Architecturally the period was distinguished by the rise of many splendid buildings, cathedrals, churches, and colleges in the distinctive light and lofty Perpendicular manner. To take only a few, we may be grateful for the splendid town church of St. Nicholas, King's Lynn, King's College Chapel at Cambridge, St. George's Chapel, Windsor, and Henry VII's Chapel, Westminster.

The century saw the foundation of Eton College, and the building of the first colleges of Oxford and Cambridge. Many fine manor-houses had arisen by the end of the century, especially in Somerset, Dorset, and Wiltshire, such as Great Chalfield, Wiltshire(*146*). The gilds increased, and a large number of chantry chapels were built, in which masses were celebrated for the souls of the dead.

There was a great development in commerce; money was more generally used, but not yet understood as only being a medium of exchange. In Henry IV's time it was said: "Since the year 1351, 300 pennies had been struck from the lb Tower of silver, and 45 nobles, of 6*s*. 8*d*. each, from the lb Tower of gold." In 1411 they tried making 360 pennies and 50 nobles from the same quantities of gold and silver, but found that this simple method of accumulating wealth was a bad financial policy.

COSTUME

As in our chapters on the other centuries, we will begin by turning to the costume of the period, which reflects its extravagance and licence. Fig. *111* shows how each garment was a little more exaggerated, and every fashion still more extraordinary, than in the preceding century.

Take, for example, the first man in the picture. His capuchon has entirely lost its usefulness as a hood, and is no longer even a turban, but with a stiff, circular brim has become a hat with a crest to it and a long tail of stuff, originally the liripipe,

198

hanging down the back. This piece of stuff was often so long that it could be wound around the neck, and yet still trailed on the ground behind. The pelisse is very full, and the sleeves are wide and long enough to touch the ground. The collar is high, fastening right up to the chin.

In the early years of the fifteenth century some of the men had their hair dressed in a very peculiar way. Look at the second man in the illustration, and you will see that his hair, although allowed to grow very thickly on the crown, is cut round his head above the ears, leaving the part below shaved quite bare. This style is generally supposed to have been adopted so that the head should be cool and comfortable inside the helmet, while the top of the head would still be protected by the thick locks on the crown.

This man wears a very full and pleated surcoat, edged with fur, and belted in tightly round the waist. Men at this time exaggerated their figures as much as their clothes, and many not only tightened in their waists but wore their tunics stiffened out into a globular shape over the chest, which still further accentuated the waist-line. Look at brasses and pictures of this period, and you will see the curious shape of many of the male figures. The breast-plate in fifteenth-century armour was also moulded to the same globular form. The sleeves of this surcoat are stuffed out until they resemble bolsters, and are full and stiff, and gathered in at the wrist. The shoes are even more pointed than before, and sometimes so long as to necessitate fastening the points up to the knee with small jewelled chains.

The first lady of the picture wears one of the monstrous head-dresses of this period, very high and pointed, with a velvet roll round the head, enriched with a jewelled ornament in the front. Notice the fine muslin or gauze veil, and the curious stiffened muslin over the face and round the neck. These head-dresses were very costly affairs, made of gold or silver tissue, or of wonderful brocades, often covered with jewels and golden ornamentation. They were of many different shapes, although there is only space for two in the picture. One favourite head-dress, besides those shown here, was in the form of a large horn, curving upwards on either side of the head. A fine veil was then stretched from point to point, and hung down the back; this type is very often seen, both on brasses and in old manuscripts. Notice this lady's surcoat, which almost resembles a dress, as we understand the word; while her cotte of blue is so nearly hidden that it has begun to suggest a modern petticoat.

The second lady also wears an extraordinary head-dress— of blue and purple velvet, worked in gold and pearls. These wonderful erections must have been not only very costly but extremely cumbersome and uncomfortable.

All fashionable dress in this century was brilliant in colour, costly in material, and generally extreme in form, suited to the habits of a rich and idle upper class. Much time and thought were needed to arrange it, and it must have greatly hampered the wearer's movements—for example, the lady's heavy ermine cloak and the trailing fur-trimmed surcoat.

The little maid attending this lady is dressed in very much the same way as were the people of the middle class—the same type of dress as was worn by the noble ladies, but considerably simplified—and on her head is still the wimple and hood of earlier times.

The next figure, a knight, shows how much more complete armour has become. Body, arms, and legs are now encased in steel, and the chain-mail hauberk beneath scarcely appears. The helmet carried by this man is of a very usual type, known as a "salade". It is so formed that it fits down over the "men-tonnière", or chin-piece, and this covers all the vital parts of the neck. It has a visor, which can be raised at will. The large helmet, or "heaume", is still used, as in the preceding century, for pageants or tournaments.

Notice, too, that the knight wears no surcoat. This garment was no longer worn over armour in the early and middle parts of the fifteenth century; but, after this date, its place was taken by the "tabard", a much looser tunic, with wide elbow-sleeves.

It must not be thought that the various forms of costume and armour displayed in our plates were the only types seen during their respective centuries. In a period of a hundred years there is time for many changes in style. So the garments illustrated have, as nearly as possible, been taken from the middle years of the epoch; and if in imagination we bridge the gaps between, and think of the earlier examples as altering, and being amplified, and changing, step by step, until they culminate in a typical example of the following century, we shall gain some idea of the growth of dress through the ages.

DETAILS OF DRESS

Our next illustration(*139*) has been inserted because we think that our feminine readers may be interested in the way medieval dresses were cut. It shows many small details of dress —things that in pictures we hardly notice, but that, nevertheless, make all the difference between one century and another.

Let us take first No. 1, the centre garment. This is the medieval cotte or under-tunic, the principal garment from the twelfth until the sixteenth century. Later, it gradually changed into the petticoat, and the surcoat over it altered until it became an entire dress. As time went on, the shape naturally changed. In the fifteenth century the bodice was tight, and the skirt much

139   Details of Medieval Dress

1	Under-tunic	6	Type of bag
2	Surcoat	7–10	Men's bags
3	Man's tunic	11	Medieval whip
4	Hood or head-dress	12	Chaplet used during ceremonies
5	Various kinds of shoes	13	Dressing-Comb

fuller than in the twelfth and thirteenth; but the design of the garment was always the same, until it finally disappeared.

No. 2 is a pattern of the earliest form of surcoat. In the twelfth century this was called a bliaut, and was cut very much as a sleeveless tunic. The neck was rounded, and was rather lower than that of the cotte. In the thirteenth-century costume illustration(45), the little girl is wearing one of the usual pattern.

In the late thirteenth and early fourteenth centuries the surcoat took the place of the bliaut. Its early form was like the pattern given here, but its shape altered a great deal with the passage of years. Look at the first lady in the fifteenth-century illustration (111), and you will see that the surcoat has become a complete dress, and the cotte has almost turned into a petticoat. The surcoat of the second lady is not the same. It is sleeveless, and clearly shows the cotte beneath.

Pattern No. 3 shows a man's tunic, worn by all men in the twelfth century, and in the same form by peasants until the sixteenth century, when breeches and doublet came into common use. Worn by the Norman nobles, the tunic fell below the knee, sometimes to the ankle, and was full, girt into the waist with a belt.

As the centuries passed, its shape and length varied. In the fifteenth century there was nothing left of it below the waist but a frill, and the long chausses were fastened to the waist with points or little knots of ribbon. In Henry VIII's reign the tunic finally gave place to the doublet, with breeches and hosen beneath.

No. 4 gives the pattern of a very early form of head-dress, one that was in general use until the sixteenth century. The capuchon, or hood, must have been a useful and comfortable garment. The cape pulled well down over the shoulders; and in stormy weather the hood would be warm and cosy round the neck and ears. Peasants kept to the capuchon in its early form; but among the nobles it was altered and twisted and worn in many ways, until it ended as very little else but unnecessary ornamentation to a hat. We can see its various stages in the illustrations of the fourteenth- and fifteenth-century men's costumes.

No. 5 gives various kinds of shoe. In medieval times shoes

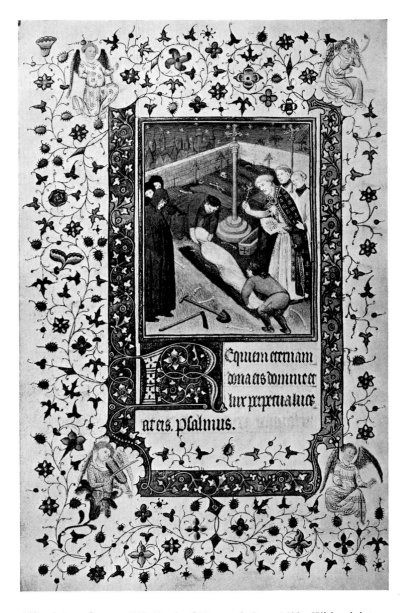

140 A Page from an MS. Book of Hours of about 1400. With miniature
of a Burial

141 A Town Garden with square beds. The owner gives directions

142 A Rose Hedge round the Castle Walks

were made of thick cloth, felt, or soft leather, or sometimes of velvet. They were without raised heels, and in the twelfth century were cut to the shape of the foot. Among the nobles of the fourteenth century the fashion arose of wearing pointed shoes. This fashion became more and more exaggerated, until, in the fifteenth century, shoes were so tapered and so ridiculously long that, as we have already explained, it became necessary to fasten up the points. Watch any fashion, and you will find that it starts as being useful, is then beautified, and finally exaggerated until it becomes ridiculous, and at last is swept clean away and replaced by another. So it was with shoes.

Suddenly, at the end of the fifteenth century, these grotesque points gave place to shoes as wide in the toe as they had before been narrow. A, B, and C show the development of the point. A is a twelfth-century shoe, B that of the thirteenth and four-teenth, and C is a shoe of the early fifteenth century, the last exaggeration of the style.

Peasants' shoes were sometimes cut in thick cloth, and did not keep out the mud and wet in the winter (p. 184), so D shows the kind of heavy wooden clog worn in bad weather.

E is a clog, also of wood, in use among well-to-do people in the fourteenth century.

Hanging on the sleeves of pattern No. 1 are two ladies' handbags of the fourteenth century. Such bags were an im-portant part of a woman's ensemble, and generally contained a little book of devotions; the cover of the book itself was called a chemise.

No. 6 is another type of bag carried at the same period. This was of a long funnel-like shape, embroidered and stiffened at the bottom, and was generally carried wound round the arm or into the belt.

Nos. 7, 8, 9, and 10 are men's bags, and in Nos. 7 and 9 you will see how the dagger is carried through a strap on the bag, especially made for it.

On the belt of No. 10 is also carried a sheath, often containing writing implements, a knife, and any article useful in whatever trade the owner might practise.

No. 11 is a medieval whip, as illustrated in many old drawings. It has a wooden handle, and three cords for a lash, each weighted at the end with a small piece of lead—a rather cruel weapon.

No. 12 is a chaplet, worn around the head both by men and by women, on occasions of ceremony, during the twelfth, thirteenth, and fourteenth centuries. The one illustrated is made of metal, either gold or silver, and is probably jewelled. Sometimes fresh flowers were used in making these chaplets, and the effect must then have been very charming, especially on young heads.

No. 13 is a dressing-comb. All medieval combs of which we have any record are of this shape. They were made in ivory, horn, bone, and even wood, and were often beautifully carved and fashioned.

Small articles such as these were, in olden times, much less easily obtained than they are now, and each was some craftsman's individual work. Instead of being turned out cheaply by the thousand from a machine, each bore the stamp of the love and labour expended on it.

MERCHANTS AND FOREIGN TRADE

The next everyday thing is the ship; and fig. *143* shows one of the fifteenth century. This is clearly a great improvement on the rather clumsy single-masted boat, with one square sail, that we showed in our fourteenth-century chapter. Ruskin describes a ship as "one of the loveliest things man ever made, and one of the noblest". The fifteenth-century ship was equally beautiful and useful. It owed its development to the rapid growth of industry and foreign trade.

English Merchant Adventurers bought and sold in European ports from the Baltic to the Mediterranean. The fifteenth-century sailors were worthy forerunners of the wonderful seamen of the sixteenth century. Christopher Columbus sailed west in 1492, with only three small ships, and discovered the West Indies, and afterwards America. Cabot sailed from Bristol in 1497; and Vasco da Gama, in the same year, set sail from the Tagus around the Cape of Good Hope for India. This was an epoch-making voyage. There had been, from very early times, a trade between the Mediterranean and India, goods being taken overland to the Red Sea on the line of the modern Suez Canal. This trade had been stopped by the Sultans of Egypt; so European navigators put their heads together, and sailed south down the west coast of Africa until they found

143　A Ship of the time of Christopher Columbus

their way round the Cape, and so into the Indian Ocean. This remained the ordinary trade route until the Suez Canal was made; and it diverted the trade from the Mediterranean ports and very greatly damaged their commerce.

SHIPS

Now all this development of trade meant a corresponding improvement of ships; which brings us back to our illustration of a fifteenth-century vessel. But ships of that age were still very small; Columbus's flagship, the *Santa Maria*, was only about 93 feet in length, with a breadth of 25 feet. A model of her was made in Spain in 1893, and sailed across the Atlantic to the Chicago Exhibition. She took thirty-six days, her maximum speed was $6\frac{1}{2}$ knots, and we are told that she pitched horribly. Compared with a liner of to-day, she was the merest cockleshell; and it needed brave men to sail her into the unknown seas.

207

Our illustration shows a boat rigged on much the same lines as the *Santa Maria*. There are three masts: the foremast, main-mast, and mizzen. The first has a square foresail; the mainmast, a mainsail and topsail; and the mizzen has a three-cornered lateen or leg-of-mutton sail. This latter is the first appearance of what was the typical Eastern or Mediterranean sail; and it is worth a little consideration, since it has had an interesting history through the centuries, and still remains on the mizzen of a modern sailing-ship as the spanker or driver. The Eastern ship was lateen-rigged on all masts, and now began to borrow the Northern square sail, while we adopted the idea of the lateen, and used it on the mizzen; and from this mingling of ideas the modern ship was evolved. The Arabs still stick to the old leg-of-mutton type. All the sails were now cut much fuller, and bellied out before the wind, and were made smaller by taking off pieces at the bottom, called "bonnets", instead of reefing the sail by gathering it up. Bowlines were used to set them properly.

The three masts shown in our drawing introduced many variations in the rigging; more stays are introduced, and the braces of the yards are sometimes worked off these.

So far as the hull is concerned, the forecastle, instead of being a square platform, is pointed in shape, and is becoming beak-like, and is altogether trimmer than in the fourteenth century. Carvel-building was another introduction from the East, and consisted of building the boat of planks, with their joints butting up against one another, instead of clinker-built as before, with the edges overlapping. Skids were placed along the sides, and the stern built up into a regular poop.

One thing to be remembered is that, up to 1628, the tonnage of a boat was reckoned by the number of tuns of wine which could be stowed away in her, and a tun equalled 42 cubic feet; after that date it was reckoned by taking the length of the keel and multiplying it by the greatest breadth of beam, and by the depth, and dividing the result by 100.

Fig. *144* gives some additional details of fifteenth-century ships drawn from the *Warwick Pageant* MS. in the British Museum, of which a facsimile has been published. This deals, in the most wonderful way, with the birth, life, and death of Richard Beauchamp, Earl of Warwick, 1389–1439. There are

144   Ship details from the *Warwick Pageant* MS. in
the British Museum

53 outline drawings in the MS., which must have been made some time after the Earl's death.

THE GROWTH OF INDUSTRY

Commerce and industry at home kept pace with the growth of foreign trade; the manufacture of cloth prospered, and coal, iron, and tin were mined.

Coal had been mined, and iron mined and smelted, from a very early period. Even during the Roman occupation the trade was of sufficient importance to maintain gilds; and in the twelfth century several monasteries depended for their revenues on the iron mines they worked. The ore was smelted in large furnaces made of charcoal covered with a beehive shape of clay with vent holes at the bottom, one of which allowed the molten metal silting through the fire to run away down into a channel cut in the earth. Bellows made of skins were employed to keep the furnace glowing. Two sheds were used, one for smelting and one for forging, and these were worked by a couple or more men who, having obtained a licence to work iron in certain districts, moved about, working the iron in one place until it was exhausted, and then moving on to another. In the Forest of Dean, the miners held their own court and tried and punished their own offenders. This custom lasted until the end of the eighteenth century.

Tin and lead were worked in much the same way as iron; and from the thirteenth to the early fifteenth century they supported powerful industries, each with its own gild and court to try offenders, strong enough to inflict punishment that none dared dispute. In the Mendip Hills, a miner who stole lead was condemned to have his tools all put together in his house or working shed and to "set fyer yn all about him", he then to be banished for evermore from that occupation.

Silver was mined until the fifteenth century, when the mines were said to be exhausted and the industry died. Copper is believed to have been generally imported from Europe; but tin and iron were exported, and all these industries led to the development of foreign trade.

THE DEVELOPMENT OF THE HOUSE

We must now leave merchants and miners, and begin our survey of the fifteenth-century house. The one illustrated dates

1 Entrance courtyard
2 Entrance porch
3 Screens
4 The Hall
5 Winter parlour
6 Bake- and brew-houses
7 Cellar
8 Bay windows
9 Inner court

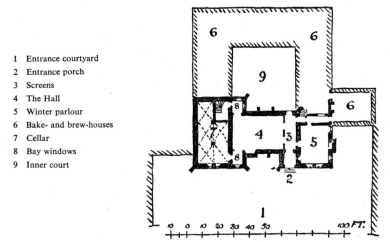

145   Plan of Fifteenth-Century Manor-House

from 1480. It is particularly interesting because it shows that a new middle class of people was springing up, who had benefited by the fratricidal strife between the nobles during the Wars of the Roses. For this new class, doubtless, Caxton published his *Book of Good Manners*, so that they might become polite. The impoverished nobility married the daughters of prosperous merchants, and the latter acquired land and gentility.

Fig. *145* is of the plan of a fifteenth-century manor-house. At 1 was the entrance courtyard, around which were grouped the stables and other offices necessary to a house of this size. There would be a gatehouse at the point of entry, defended by good doors, with a moat around the outside. There might be another yard, with barns and farm buildings, within the outer enclosure. At 2 is the entrance porch, leading to the screens, 3, which are at the end of the hall, 4. At 5 is the winter parlour—a new room, the uses of which are described later on. It must be noticed that, as a result of this addition, the pantry and buttery have been put in a new place, and no longer occupy the same position as in the thirteenth and fourteenth centuries, next the screens. These, with the kitchen and other offices such as bake- and brewhouses, are now at 6, grouped round an inner court at 9. The cellar is still at 7 at the end of the hall, and the solar is over it on the first floor. At this, the dais end of the hall,

211

146   A House of the time of Edward IV, based on Great Chalfield,
Wiltshire ("Perpendicular" style)

are new additions in the form of bay windows at 8, 8. Here they
do not go up the whole height of the hall, but have small rooms
over on the first floor, which probably served as bedrooms.
There is another chamber on the first floor, over the winter
parlour at 5; and the staircase at the back led up to this chamber, the minstrels' gallery over the screens, and other bedrooms
over the pantry and buttery.

So our house is becoming much more like a modern house;
there is a good deal more accommodation in it and, notably,
there are many more small rooms, in which the various members
of the family could enjoy greater privacy than had hitherto been
possible.

Our illustration(*146*) depicts the exterior of the fifteenth-
century manor-house. The design of this house is quite Gothic
in character; but it shows that its builders were beginning to
balance their designs, and make them symmetrical—that
is, one side like the other. Yet this house owes much of its
charm to the fact that it is not so absolutely symmetrical as
became the fashion in the sixteenth century. The original house
on which this drawing is founded is Great Chalfield in the stone
district of Wiltshire, in which there are many fine Tudor houses.
It was built by Thomas Tropenell, probably towards the end of

the reign of Henry VI, and, in spite of the loss of a wing, forms a charming group with its moat and tiny stone-bellcote church.

It is evident that far greater attention is being paid to comfort, and less to defence. There are plenty of windows; the inhabitants want light and air. The battlements have disappeared. We now come across, for the first time, a new type of arch. In the twelfth century we had the semicircular type, while those of the next two centuries were pointed and turned in from two centres. A pair of compasses will soon demonstrate what is meant. In the fifteenth we get a flatter type, set out from four centres.

The hall remains as the central feature, and is so expressed on the outside; but the house itself looks more connected, and is no longer a collection of different buildings huddled up together. The hall is still a big lofty place, going up to the roof, and so cutting the house in two halves, the general arrangement of which is described in connection with the plan (*145*).

To judge by the exterior, the solar on the left-hand side and the chamber on the right were the two most important rooms after the hall, as they are marked externally by very beautiful oriel windows. These are a new essay in design; and one feels that whoever was responsible for them must have been pleased with his work. The bay windows to the hall, which are another new feature, do not show on the outside as such because of the little rooms over. Access to these was gained by a newel staircase at the back of the cellar at 7 on plan, through a doorway out of one of the bays at 8. Fig. *149* shows one of these bedrooms.

The chamber over the winter parlour must have been used as a spare bedroom; and we have seen how this began in the fourteenth century. Another development appears to be the provision of a loft in the roof, over the hall, to be used as a dormitory for the retainers. People generally were making themselves more comfortable.

This house, the last we shall illustrate in Vol. I, was built of stone. In the house shown in fig. *73* brick was used, and the two illustrated in figs. *107* and *110* framed up in oak. It should be noted how different materials need different architectural treatments. The wise architect does not try to make a timber house look as if it were built of stone; nor does he find any joy in transporting slates from Wales to roof a house in a district where good tiles can be made. Nature in the kindliest way has provided in every part of the country building materials that tune in with the landscape, last better than those imported, and were at one time cheaper.

Fig. *147* illustrates the solar or chamber in a fifteenth-century house, still used, like that of the thirteenth, as the private sitting- and bedroom of the lord. The oriel window to this room is shown in the illustration of the exterior of the house, on the extreme left of the picture(*146*), balancing the chamber oriel on the right.

The drawing of the interior demonstrates what a charming addition the oriel was to the room itself. The plain panels at the sides are in the thickness of the wall, and beyond these come the stone mullions of the window. The roof has a very beautiful little fan vault. Think of the setting out and care that went to make it. The timber roof to the chamber is a development of the simpler type, without a hammer-beam. This is called a collar-beam roof, from the collar, or tie, across over the curved braces, which are fitted in between the principal rafters and the collar. These braces follow the same four centred lines as the arches to the heads of the windows. The curved timbers, fitted in between the purlins and abutting on the principals, are called wind-braces. The walls under are plastered and covered with tapestry.

THE WINTER PARLOUR

Fig. *148* illustrates the winter parlour, situated at 5 on the plan of the fifteenth-century house. This room began to make its appearance at the end of the fifteenth century, and was the forerunner of the modern dining-room. As its name shows, the room was first used by the family to take their meals in during the cold weather, though probably they still dined in the hall on great occasions and during the summer. Again we note the desire for greater privacy. As time goes on, we shall find that the winter parlour becomes the dining-room, and the hall is only used as a place of entrance, the retainers having their meals in the servants' hall or kitchen.

147   The Solar of a Fifteenth-Century House ("Perpendicular" style)

The drawing also illustrates a new style of wood panelling, which came in about this time, and was called the linen-fold pattern, because the panels were moulded so that the design looked like folded linen.   The moulding was run out with

215

148   The Winter Parlour

hollow and round planes, and the ends carved in a variety of
beautiful ways. The panelling itself was much thinner, and
more like a door than it had been. In the Liberate Rolls of
Henry III's time, in the thirteenth century, we read of rooms
being wainscoted in wood, which means panelling; but it would
have been heavier in character, rather like a church screen,
or window, with wooden panels filled in between bars. The
ceiling in this drawing has moulded beams showing the floor-
boards over, which was the general method in medieval times.
Beautiful plaster ceilings were to come in during the next
century.

The furniture, chairs and chests are still rather more like the
furnishings of a church than anything we now associate with a

149   A Fifteenth-Century Bedchamber

house; yet the whole character of the room is becoming much more modern.

The next illustration (*149*) is of one of the smaller bed-chambers to which we referred on page 213. Some of these bed-chambers had rush-strewn floors, and there was a pretty custom of hanging the walls with freshly cut boughs, to make the room cool and fragrant. Until tapestry came into general use, the walls were painted with varied decorations, often scenes from some romance. Window-glass was now in general use; and the vividly coloured panes depicted scenes and histories.

SPINNING AND WEAVING

We have often explained how in medieval times people were nearly self-sufficient; and in our illustration of a fifteenth-century solar we show the ladies of the house spinning and weaving. They are producing sheets, blankets, and cloth for an entire household.

Cloth was prepared as follows. The fleece, after the shearing, was thoroughly scoured and washed, then dyed. Teasing was the next operation, and consisted of pulling the dry dyed fleece into fluff. Carding followed, and this is what the lady on the left is doing. Nowadays one has two cards like flat square hair-brushes fitted with barbed-wire teeth, the ends of which turn up towards the handle; and the fluff, being put on to these, is drawn from one to the other so as to be arranged as lengthwise as possible for spinning.

Spinning-wheels(97) did not come into use with distaff until the sixteenth century; the right-hand lady in fig. *147* is using a spindle. It must be remembered that all thread, yarn, and string is made by twisting up wool or similar material. The carded wool is tied on to the distaff in front; and from this a little is pulled out and twisted as it is pulled with finger and thumb, and one end tied on the spindle. The latter is then twisted sharply, and held against something to prevent it unspinning. When it is released, the twist given by the spindle runs up the thread, which all the time is being gradually pulled out from the distaff. The thread is then wound round the spindle, and so on again.

Now for weaving, which is just like darning, where a needleful of wool is stretched across the hole from edge to edge: this would be called the "warp" in weaving. If a stocking is being mended, the second row of threads is darned across the first row, first under and then over. In weaving, this second row is the "weft". All looms are constructed to work on this principle; but, as you must weave long lengths, it is necessary to be able to roll it up as you go along; so the warp is stretched between two rollers. Instead of the darning-needle, a shuttle is employed, and the thread, wound on a bobbin placed in this, is thrown from side to side. A shuttle, being bigger than a needle, could not be worked in and out over one thread of the warp and under the next; so one set of threads is depressed and the other raised by being passed through loops, which are worked by treadles and called headles. This gives the space for the shuttle to be thrown through, and there may be many treadles and headles which, by moving different sets of threads, allow patterns to be formed. Then there is a swinging arrangement which has a reed or comb at the end, through which the warp threads are passed; and this is banged down hard against the work as it is being woven, to pack the weft up tight.

TAPESTRY AND THE WOOL-TRADE

The first tapestry was woven at Arras; hence the name for it that Shakespeare uses; Polonius, of course, is stabbed by Hamlet behind the arras. Much earlier, in Edward II's reign, we read that £30 was paid to Thomas de Hebenith, mercer of London, for a great hanging of wool, woven with figures of the king and earl, for the king's service in his hall on solemn occasions.

The wool trade in England was one of her greatest industries; and the fame of English wool extended throughout Europe. By the twelfth century weavers in the large cities had formed themselves into gilds and were a powerful and wealthy community. The Fullers, too, and all the various branches of the trade, formed gilds and framed rules and regulations for the advancement of their business. Many kinds of cloth were made, and Lincoln in the twelfth century was famous for a fine and expensive scarlet cloth, while the cheaper and coarse woollen cloth, called burel, was manufactured in Cornwall. This was used chiefly by the poor; and in 1246 the Sheriff of London ordered a thousand ells of burel for presentation to the poor of London.

Coverlets or counterpanes of wool-like rugs were used as bed coverings and were made at Winchester. Many cloths took their names from the places where they were originally made. Thus Kersey made kerseymere; Kendal was made at the town of that name; and the coverlets of wool made at Winchester were called Chalons; for originally they had come from Châlons-sur-Marne. At Norwich was made a thick woollen stuff, used for hangings as well as for tapestry.

In the later Middle Ages, the activity and prosperity of the wool trade led to a crop of lovely buildings in the centres of its activity. In the Cotswolds, there is the delightful unspoilt town of Chipping Campden; and there and at Winchcombe, Northleach, Cirencester, and Fairford, we find noble "wool-churches". Stamford, one of the pleasantest old towns in England, largely owes its charm to the former trade in wool; and, over in the west Midlands, Leominster was another centre. Some of the wool merchants' names have come down to us; for instance, that of William Grevel, whose fine house still stands in Campden High Street; Fairford was the home of the Tame family. The magnificent church of Lavenham, the little Tudor weaving

219

town in mid-Suffolk, is a wool church; largely rebuilt in the fifteenth century by the generous co-operation of the Earl of Oxford and Thomas Spryng, a wealthy clothier. His own and his son's badges are carved in different parts of the building, which is noble and stately and full of fine craftsmanship. One of these old wool merchants had inscribed on his monument:

I thank God and ever shall
It was the sheep that payed for all.

Much exquisite work, many wonderful scenes were woven into tapestries; and nobles, when travelling, often took them in their baggage train, and hung them in their temporary apartments, wherever these might be. Froissart describes a pageant in Paris, given for Queen Isabelle in 1399, in which one whole street was hung with tapestry and also canopied with silk.

GARDENS AND FLOWERS

Now what about gardens? We have said a great deal about houses, but have scarcely referred to gardens. Medieval people were fond of flowers; and many charming manuscript pictures explain how their idea of the places in which to grow them developed and took shape. During the troubled early times gardens were confined to monasteries, and were of a severely practical form, allowing great space to the orchard, the vegetable garden, and the medicinal herb garden. But flowers grew in them all, and the list of plants cultivated is very long. By the fifteenth century we find regularly fair-sized enclosures, with some trees and raised rectangular beds, and subdivisions of trellis, within a high wall or wattle fence, and often an elaborate fountain and shady branch-woven arbours. People played music in these shady retreats, and, as Chaucer's poem shows, they were not averse from a picnic (p. 193). Raised banks served as seats; they were covered with turf, and, except in the hottest weather, might have seemed painfully damp to us. Fig. *141* shows a spacious town garden, but it has a somewhat monotonous layout. The rose hedge round the castle walls seems a praiseworthy attempt to make a stony desert blossom.

GLASS-PAINTERS AND GLASS-MAKERS

The passion for colour was universal; everything seems to have been gaily ornamented; and the effect of fifteenth-century

150 A May Day in a Medieval City. A cavalcade rides through the gate-
tower with green branches, also carried by a gay boating party. Note
the flagon trailing overboard and a woman washing clothes in the river

151   A Pleader addressing a Court of Law

152   A Town Shopping Street. In front, draper and grocer; at the back,
furrier and barber, with bowls as sign

rooms, with their tapestries or painted walls, their embroidered bed-hangings and windows of stained glass, must have been jewel-like. Even the church woodwork of this period shows traces of brilliant colour here and there, remnants of this vivid era.

Chaucer in his "Dreame", in the fourteenth century, thus describes his bedchamber:

> And sooth to saine my chamber was
> Full well depainted and with glas
> Were all the windows well y-glased.
> Full clere and nat a hole y-crased
> That to behold it was a joy,
> For holly all the story of Troy
> Was in the glaising y-wroughte thus.
>
> . . . . . .
>
> And all the walls of colors fine
> Were paint both text and glose
> And all the Romant of the Rose,
> My windows weren that echone
> And through the glasse the sunne came.

Chaucer, as we have seen, speaks of glass as a rare and precious commodity.

Glass was blown at a very early date. Since it was blown in a bubble, cut in half and whirled into a disk, the margin of clear glass from the centre, where it was cut off the pipe, to the edge was small. In the British Museum is a Saxon glass goblet of great beauty. Glass for windows was difficult to obtain. Craftsmen painted and stained glass for church use; in 1352 John de Lincoln and John Geddyng were given commission to procure as much glass as should be needed for the King's

153 Self-portrait of Thomas the Glass-Painter, Winchester College

chapel at Westminster. How little we know of the craftsmen who wrought these arts which we now find so delightful! Only in a few instances have their names come down to us. So we can be grateful that Thomas the glass-painter has left us a little portrait signature, his hands clasped in prayer, on his work in the east window of Winchester College Chapel (*153*); and on page 142 we mentioned the little picture of William de Brailes, with his signature, snatched by a strong angel from destruction (*91*).

"Brode" glass was made in the thirteenth century, by blowing glass in the shape of a cylinder, and then cutting it down the middle and flattening it out. But even this method did not provide very large sheets of glass; and it was not until 1772 that glass was cast in plates and so made in any size required. An amusing thirteenth-century instruction for the making of glass bottles runs as follows:

> If you wish to make bottles, this do. When you have gathered some hot glass on the end of a blow-pipe, and blown it in the form of a large bladder, swing the tube with the glass appended to it, beyond your head, as if you intended to throw it, and the neck will be stretched by this action and then separate it with a wet stick and put it in the annealing furnace.

Surrey and Sussex were great glassblowing centres; and in 1377 glasshouses or works in Chiddingfold and Guildford are mentioned. The art had been practised there since early medieval times; and kilns have been found at Alfold and Rudgwick. Venice has always been noted for its glass—Henry VIII had a fine collection of Venetian table glass; and in 1567 a glasshouse was set up in London, with Venetian workmen, for the making of Venetian crystal glass; and the name Glasshouse Street, off Piccadilly, is a reminder of the trade.

FURNITURE AND POTTERY

Fig. *154* shows a very beautiful fifteenth-century cradle. Made of oak, it was suspended on iron hooks on the insides of the buttressed posts, so that the baby could be rocked. The bottom of the cradle was formed by threading some cords through holes bored in the body. Fig. *110* shows, on the right of the picture of the hall, a fourteenth-century cradle which was so much of a rocker that a vigorous infant might have overturned it.

Fig. *155* represents a fifteenth-century jug. It shows that pottery had not made any great advances throughout the whole of the Middle Ages. Perhaps the times were too rough; so the frugal housewife gave her menfolk vessels of metal or leather, which they could not break. Times were hard, and much pottery naturally got smashed. The Ashmolean Museum has rummaged over the dump outside the old city walls of Oxford, where broken pots were flung in medieval times, and has pieced together many nice simple specimens. A

154   A Fifteenth-Century Cradle

study of the illuminated manuscripts shows a wide range of shapes—plates, cups, drug-jars, etc., decorated with simple bold patterns, very much like the traditional peasant ware you can still buy in Italy or Spain.

THE DECLINE OF HALL-LIFE

In Fig. *156* a fifteenth-century hall is illustrated, such as might have been found in a large house. A similar design of roof would have been used for the nave of a church, the hall of a college, or for the hall of one of the City Companies. We still talk of the Guild Hall, or the Fishmongers' Hall, in the City of London. The Guild Hall still remains as a hall; but the Fishmongers' Hall, being a comparatively modern building, reminds us only by its name that all the City Companies at one time

155   A Fifteenth-Century Jug of green and buff earthenware

225

156   A Hall of the Fifteenth Century ("Perpendicular" style)

had their halls. In fact, almost any medieval building seems to
have been grouped around such central feature. Nevertheless hall
life was declining; and, as trade increased and became more
specialised, it became less domestic. Callings such as those of
the carpenter, brewer, tailor, and baker, instead of being part

of the life of a big house or monastery, became separate trades, followed by independent men.

Thus, with the increase of separate trades, the number of dependants on a large estate declined, the communal life of the hall grew less, and the family dined apart. In the late fourteenth century, Piers Plowman writes:

> Elyng (Dull) is the hall
> There the lorde ne the ladye . liketh noughte to sitte
> Nor hathe uche riche a ruele . to eten bi hym-selve
> In a prive parloure . for pore mennes sake
> Or in a chambre with a chymneye . leve the chief halle
> That was made for meles . men to eten inne.

Again, in the Collection of Ordinances for the government of the Royal Household, at Eltham in 1526, we read:

> Sundrie noblemen and gentlemen and others doe muche delighte and use to dyne [dine] in corners and secret places, not repayring to the Kinges chamber or hall.

THE HAMMER-BEAM ROOF

The first thing that will strike our readers, if they have been following the development of the roofs shown in the earlier illustrations, is that our fifteenth-century example is quite a new type. The name for it is the "hammer-beam roof", so called because the beam on which the figures are standing is like the head of a hammer. In the earlier roofs, as will be seen by reference to the thirteenth- and fourteenth-century chapters, the tie-beam goes right across from the top of one side wall to the other. In the middle of this stood the king-post; and there were various struts and braces that helped to support the roof. The effect of this series of horizontal tie-beams at the level of the springing of the roof was to cut off the apparent height and prevent its full beauties being seen. So the centre of the tie-beam was cut away, leaving the hammer-beams at each side. Underneath these were fitted the curved struts. The king-post had to go, because now it had not any tie-beam to stand upon; but two posts took its place, one standing on each of the hammer-beams, and so taking weight from the principal rafters and conveying it, by means of the curved struts under, well down the walls. In between the posts, on the hammer-beams and the principal rafters, are fitted curved braces, which again have the effect of stiffening what is called the principal. The names and uses of the parts of a roof have been described on pages 115 and 116, and they remain the same. In this roof there are intermediate principals, spaced midway between those with the figures. The purlins are framed in between the principals, and carry the smaller, or common, rafters.

In the spaces left between the larger timbers there is very delicate tracery, which contrasts most pleasantly with, and lends grace to, the heavier construction. A man who could design this roof, and make it, was worthy of being called a good craftsman; and, fortunately for us, we still have many beautiful specimens of hammer-beam roofs left. The most celebrated, of course, is that over Westminster Hall, constructed in Richard II's reign (1394). This is justly considered one of the finest open-timbered Gothic roofs in existence. Though it is one of the finest, it is also one of the earliest; the fifteenth century is generally considered the period of the hammer-beam roof. Some of the great church roofs of East Anglia have two tiers of hammer-beams, one above the other; this type is known as a double hammer-beam roof. Opinions differ as to whether, from the standpoint of design, they are supreme, or whether the simpler form we illustrate in fig. *156* is preferable. There is no doubt of the fine complex craftsmanship of the double kind in such examples as Knapton and Swaffham, Norfolk, and March, Cambridgeshire, where each hammer-beam ends in an angel with outstretched pinions, so that the whole space seems filled with rushing wings. The type persisted into the next two centuries; a splendid double hammer-beam roof of the sixteenth century at the Middle Temple Hall, London, is depicted in Vol. II. There are also seventeenth-century hammer-beams in the churches of Plaxtol, Kent, and Vowchurch and Brampton Bryan, Herefordshire.

The rest of the drawing shows windows of Perpendicular design, with the screens at the end of the hall. The side walls are covered with tapestry. The costume of the minstrel, and of his audience, is the same as that described in connection with the costume plate for this century.

THE PARISH CHURCH

THE PARISH CHURCH AND THE PARISH LIFE

We can now leave the worldly side of life and turn to its religious aspect. All English people have seen hundreds of old churches. We have, in fact, seen so many that we may take them for granted, and are in danger of forgetting that they are a priceless national heritage—that is, if they escaped "restoration" by nineteenth-century vandals. We are only beginning to appreciate the treasures of our great heritage, still immense despite centuries of destruction. There are many fine books to study; but, better still, we can look at the churches themselves, where we shall find many variations in interiors and fittings.

Let us see how this came about. The first thing to understand is that the village church formed part and parcel of the medieval manor. In it both lord and villein worshipped. Since it had been founded perhaps by some pious ancestor, who had presented land for its maintenance, the lord of the manor would have the right to present to the living a man whom he considered suitable. This right still remains and is called the advowson. The chancel of the church belonged to the lord of the manor; and, because this was the sanctuary containing the altar, it was screened off. Its name was derived from *cancelli* (lattice). The chancel screen was surmounted by the rood loft, so called because of its large crucifix, or rood.

The nave and tower belonged to the people. This joint ownership is still found. At Hemel Hempstead Church, in Hertfordshire, the Ecclesiastical Commissioners are responsible for the maintenance of the chancel, while the Church Council look after the nave and transepts. Supposing that some of our readers go to see the ironwork on the porch door of the church at Eaton Bray, in Bedfordshire, they may be surprised to find a large hook hanging on the wall of the nave. This is a fire-hook, used in the old days to pull the burning thatch off cottage roofs. The hook was kept in the nave because it was a place in which the villagers would be sure to find it.

Sometimes a plough was kept within the tower arch for use on Plough Monday after Epiphany, so that it could be blessed in the work that it was to do for the sowing.

Frequently manorial courts were held in the nave, since a

229

church could own both land and villeins; and these had to have a place where they could meet the church reeve, who was the medieval churchwarden, or the sidesmen who looked after the sides, or parts of the manor. Then there was the business of tithes to be settled. The scot ale was a dinner given to tenants who came to pay their rent, or scot—hence "scot-free" as an expression.

Sometimes the church reeve received gifts of barley, which he brewed into ale and sold at a profit towards the upkeep of the church. This gave rise to what were known as church ales. Sometimes the length of the chain, which was used to measure off the allotments in the common fields, was marked off in the nave. Inquests were held there; even to-day we use the church door as a place to display all kinds of legal notices. The pulpit was placed in the nave, because it was here that the priest preached to his people; but, in case he lost count of the time, an hour-glass was placed at his side as a reminder.

Pews were not introduced until the fifteenth century. Figs. *157* and *158* show what opportunities the poupée, or poppy heads, forming the terminals to the ends, gave the carvers for indulging their sense of fun.

157 Poupée
(Poppy) Head

Sometimes disputes were settled in the church. The parties being assembled, Mass was celebrated, and the disputants swore by the Lord's Body that they were telling the truth, and their neighbours were witnesses. School was held in the church porch or in a chamber over it. Here the first part of the marriage service was read. Chaucer says of his "Good Wif of bisidé Bathe":

Boold was hir face, and fair, and reed of hewe,
She was a worthy womman al hir lyve;
Housbondes at chirché dore she haddé fyve.

We saw when describing Anglo-Saxon England ("Everyday Life" Series, IV) how the church tower was often used as a residence. Even in the Middle Ages the tower was a place from which watch could be kept; and it was battlemented so as to make it a strong and secure refuge in times of trouble.

Fairs were held in the church-yards. All this may sound a little shocking to modern ears; and we must leave our readers to decide which is better; the old or the new. In olden days the churches were used for a variety of purposes; and it is obvious the people loved them or they would not have made them so beautiful. To-day they seem forlorn as one tiptoes round

158 Poupée (Poppy) Head

on a weekday, and the quiet is only broken as our pennies clatter into the alms-box. But, never pass an old parish church if you have the time to explore it. We have already referred (pp. 65–6, 131–2) to the conditions of manorial life; and Mr. Bennett, of St. John's College, Cambridge, in his great study of the subject, has depicted the lives of the village folk and the part the church played in them.

MUSIC AND SONG

Music, played on many different occasions, did much to add zest and joy to the life of the Middle Ages. We think of the frequent part-singing, the solemn chants, organ-accompanied in cathedrals—some of the huge illuminated service books have the notes for the singers running beside the words. On the other hand, we must not forget the light-hearted lays of the wandering troubadours, and the improvised sagas of the castle minstrels. From manuscripts and carvings we see that medieval people used a wide range of instruments (*159*); but they were not combined into anything like a modern orchestra, though, to judge by the pictures, they did play several *in concert*, as early as Saxon times. As Chaucer noted

159   Music players: rebec, harp, shawn, and gittern

in his *Hous of Fame*, they grouped the stringed instruments together; and these would accompany the voice; then separately the wind players; and lastly the men of brass mostly for royal or warlike occasions. No doubt they made a "cheerful noise", but it is hard to tell if their efforts would have appealed to us, or if they would have enjoyed, shall we say, a Beethoven Symphony. There are many representations of companies playing—often an angelic band—such as we see on the front of the minstrels' gallery in Exeter cathedral, with twelve players, and in the capitals at Beverley Minster; but careful authorities warn us that this is unlikely to mean that all such instruments played together; the artists—carvers, or painters—just combined all the musical devices they knew in the spirit of the 150th Psalm: "Let everything that hath breath, praise the Lord." Many of these medieval instruments have really splendiferous names: the rotte, a small primitive harp; the gittern and citole, early guitars; the mandore and lute: the psaltery and dulcimer, kinds of zither: then, in the viol family, the crowd, rebec, and one-string humstrum. The organistrum and symphony were stringed, played by turning a handle, rather like a hurdy-gurdy. For wind, we have, as types of the pipe, the recorder and shawn, both sometimes double, and in the trumpet family, the horn, bugle, bumbard, buzine, and clarion. Our old friend the bagpipe, or cornemuse, was well to the fore,

160   A Jester

232

and of course the organ, either positive or the smaller portative one, to be carried about. Do you fancy hanging it round your neck, blowing with one hand and playing with the other? There were also cymbals, clappers, triangles, timbrels, or tambourines, and drums; the twin kettledrums (*99*) were called nakers. A player would clash two hand-bells; and David often appears in manuscripts seated, with two hammers hitting varying numbers of chime-bells; for as many as fifteen they had two players. Often three or four minstrels are shown performing in their gallery, while the lord and his family dine in state below. Tumblers would swing on swords, and performing animals dance, to pipe and drum, or viol; knights jousted to the sound of clarion and nakers. Among the marginal drawings of the Bodleian *The Romance of Alexander*, there occurs twice a row of ten music-players, who here at any rate have certainly got strings, wind, and percussion all playing at the same time. They seem to be enjoying themselves hugely, tootling, thrumming, or banging away, and there is even a little dog, who really looks as if it had been trained to go round with the bag.

MONASTERIES AND MONASTIC LIFE

Our illustration(*162*) is the plan, and fig. *161* a bird's-eye view, of a Carthusian monastery. The buildings of this Order have been selected for our illustration, because they show at a glance that a quite different sort of life was led in them from that in the Benedictine monastery illustrated in our chapter on the twelfth century. We have described this Order as being very largely responsible for the advance of civilisation and the arts of peace in those early warlike times. The Cistercians were great farmers, and largely responsible for bringing back into cultivation the land wasted in the north by the Conqueror; the Franciscans and Dominicans were preachers; all these Orders lived busy, useful lives, and were a great civilising influence. The Carthusians, on the other hand, lived isolated from the world and one another; and the lay brothers did all the work; it was only on Sundays and feast-days that the fathers dined together, and even then conversation was not allowed. Their lives were passed in little separate houses, each with its own garden surrounded by high walls; and their two meals a

161　Bird's-eye view of a Carthusian Monastery,
based on Mount Grace Priory, Yorkshire

day were brought and put through a hatch, the first at 10 a.m. and the other at 4.30 p.m. This hatch, which is shown on the plan of one of their houses, at the right-hand side of the door, was so contrived with an angle that the person placing food in it from the outside could not be seen by the father inside. The monks rose at 5.45, and spent ten hours in devotion, ten hours in sleep and work, and four hours' recreation in digging, or reading, a day. They wore a hair shirt next the skin, with an outer robe of white serge; and their food consisted of fish, eggs, milk, cheese, bread, butter, fruit, and vegetables. This was how they passed their lives; and, when they died, they were buried in the garth of the inner cloister, so that their final resting-place was a constant reminder to their fellows to prepare to be ready to follow them. It seems to have been a gloomy conception of life and its opportunities and responsibilities—not nearly so fine as that of the Benedictines; but, in the rough-and-tumble of the Middle Ages, it doubtless attracted men broken by the storm and stress of the times.

162 Plan of the Carthusian Monastery, shown as fig. 161, and a detail of one of the Houses

1 Entrance
2 Outer court
3 Guests' quarters
4 Stables
5 Barns
6 Outer court
7 Chapter or monks' parliament
8 Sacristan's cell
9 Prior's cell
10 Prior's garden
11 Monk's frater or refectory
12 Kitchens
13 Lay brothers' frater
14 Inner cloister
15 Burying-place

Now for a consideration of the monastic buildings. At 1 on the plan was the entrance to the outer court at 2, around which were grouped, at 3, the quarters for the guests, and at 4 the stables for their horses, and for those of the farm attached to the monastery, and the barns were at 5. It must be remembered that a convent of monks would be in much the same position as the large households of castle and manor-house: they would grow nearly all their own meat, corn, and vegetables; make their own bread, cheese, butter, and beer, depending only on the fairs to exchange their wool, perhaps, for salt, wine, spices, and the little household oddments. So they needed large buildings. We must imagine this outer court, then, with lay brothers busy at their work, tending the horses, perhaps carting in corn; pilgrims

235

arriving on their way to some shrine, or an ecclesiastic on a mission to the prior. Here would have been the bustle of the outside world, in contrast to the quietude of the inner cloister.

The church was on the north side of the outer court, at 6, and arranged in two halves: one for the lay brothers at the west, and another to the east for the fathers, or monks. Each had a separate entrance, the lay brothers coming in from a little separate court at the west end, and the monks from the cloisters on the north side. Laymen, or the outside public, were not admitted to the church; and the fathers do not appear to have acted as parish priests, or to have preached.

The chapter, or monks' parliament, was at 7, and the sacristan who was responsible for the care of the church had a cell at 8. The prior's cell was at 9; he was the governor of the convent, and his cell commanded the entrance to the inner cloister, and he could see who came in and who went out. He had a little garden at 10. The frater, or refectory for the monks, was at 11, and the kitchens at 12; and it is probable that the lay brothers had a frater at 13.

The inner cloister was at 14, and in the central garth there was a conduit for water. At the south end of the garth was the burying-place of the monks, at 15, and around it were grouped their houses, each one standing in the corner of a small garden, separated by high walls from the others. The larger plan shows the details of the houses on the ground floor; and over each of these was one large room, or loft, used as a workshop. From the living-room a covered way led to the lavatories, built in the thickness of the walls, and projecting over a running stream. The entrance passage of the house led on to a little verandah looking on to the garden, which, with the tree-tops seen over the walls, was the monks' only outlook.

There were never more than nine Carthusian monasteries in England; the claims of the Order never met with any great response here, for there is something about the life, with its lack of usefulness, that is un-English. These drawings have been founded on careful surveys of the remains of Mount Grace Priory, a Carthusian monastery in Yorkshire, which is held to be the best English example.

A MONASTIC LIBRARY AND ITS ARCHITECTURE

The next illustration(*163*) must serve a dual purpose. In the first place, it is to show what the first library was like, and in the second the beginning of fan vaulting. It has been drawn from the cloister walk at Gloucester, which was a Benedictine monastery, and only became a cathedral in 1541 after the dissolution of the monastic bodies. Gloucester was founded at the end of the eleventh century; and, as time passed, one part after another was remodelled, or rebuilt, as the old monks tried to make their house and its church more beautiful. In this way the cloisters were begun at the end of the fourteenth century and finished about 1412.

Our sketch of a Benedictine monastery in the twelfth-century chapter was accompanied by a description of the various uses to which the different parts of the building were put; and the north walk of the cloisters was where the monks used to study. Here is a passage

163   The Cloister Library, Gloucester Cathedral

from the Rites of Durham, which also was a Benedictine foundation:

> In the north syde of the cloister, from the corner over against the church dour to the corner over against the dorter dour, was all fynely glased from the hight to the sole within a litle of the grownd into the cloister garth. And in every wyndowe iij pewes or carrells, where every one of the old monks had his carrell, severall by himselfe, that, when they had dyned, they did resorte to that place of cloister, and there studyed upon there books, every one in his carrell, all the afternonne, unto evensong tyme. This was there exercise every daie.
>
> And over against the carrells against the church wall did stande certain great almeries [cupboards] of waynscott all full of bookes, wherein did lye as well the old auncyent written Doctors of the Church as other prophane authors with dyverse other holie men's wourks, so that every one dyd studye what Doctor pleased them best, havinge the Librarie at all tymes to goe studie in besydes there carrells.

Fig. *79* shows a thirteenth-century cupboard.

In our drawing we have shown the old monks, "every one in his carrell"; the "certain great almeries", where the books were kept, stood against the wall opposite the carrels. Many rules were laid down by the Benedictine Order for the care of the books and manuscripts; and it was also usual to inscribe entreaties and curses, warning readers to treat a volume kindly. Here is one: "Quisquis quem contigerit Sit illi Iota manus" (Wash! lest touch of dirty finger On my spotless pages linger); and another: "May whoever steals or alienates this manuscript, or scratches out its title, be anathema. Amen." So when a boy, nowadays, writes in his book that no one is to purloin it, under various penalties, he is only doing what the medieval monk did before him. This care for books on the part of the old monks is quite understandable when we remember that, until the time of Caxton and the introduction of printing, they not only read the books but made them. It was in the cloister and the scriptorium that the beautiful illuminated manuscripts now in our museums were laboriously drawn out.

As to the second point of interest in the drawing, the fan vaulting, the cloister walk at Gloucester is supposed to be the

164   Sheep shearing and corn cutting   165   Cottage life in the Winter

166   A Bombardment of a Fortified City. The gunner doesn't get too near;
these early hooped guns often burst

Harleian MS. 4379

PEACE AND WAR

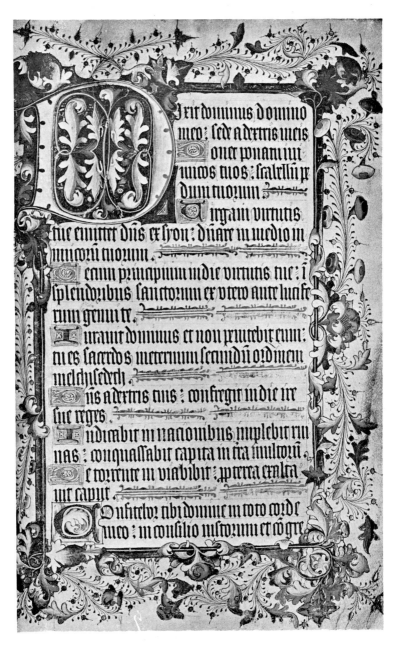

167 A Leaf from an Illuminated Psalter, about 1420. The start of Psalm cx,
"The Lord said unto my Lord," etc.

earliest example of this type. All the earlier vaults shown have consisted of semicircular or pointed tunnels, crossed by other tunnels of the same shape; and we have seen how, in the fourteenth-century lierne vault, the builders got as far as they could in this direction. Fan vaulting did away with the groin, as the line of the intersection of the tunnels was called. If we take the shape of the windows, we shall find that the section *across* the cloister, immediately in front of the fan, is the same outline as the window; but there is no groin running diagonally across the bay. The plan of the top of each fan, or conoid, is semicircular; and the plan of the whole cloister vault would be a series of semicircles, side by side, down each side, touching in the middle, and leaving diamond-shaped ceilings, more or less flat, in between. When one comes to think about it, this was the only way of escaping from the groined vault—to abolish the groin. It should be noticed that the moulded ribs are no longer of any structural use, but are carved on the face of the stone.

THE MASONS' MASTERPIECE

The next illustration(*168*) is of the fan vault over Henry VII's Chapel at Westminster Abbey. This is rightly considered the masterpiece of the masons of the Middle Ages, and must always be a source of wonder. It carries on the structural idea of the Gloucester vault(*163*). The ribs of the vault are not constructional, as they were in the thirteenth and fourteenth centuries. The whole surface is covered with a panelling, the lines of which are arched and cusped, and wreathed and interlaced in a beautiful design. Now for the construction by which this seeming miracle in stone is poised in the air. The great west window gives the shape, followed by the succession of arches which go across the chapel and take the weight of the vault. Like all arches, these are built up of wedge-shaped stones, called "voussoirs". About half-way up each side, one of these voussoirs is elongated downwards, to form the pendant of the funnel-shaped conoids which rest on the tops of the arches; and the latter at this point pass to the back of the vault. Now, if we stand at one side of the chapel, and look up at the vault on the other, we shall see that, from pendant to pendant, the two conoids meeting make

241

168 Fan Vaulting, Henry VII's Chapel, Westminster Abbey
("Perpendicular" style)

It is interesting to discover how the principle underlying these fan vaults came into being. We have seen that we owe the fan vaults as such to Gloucester, which gave us that great English style, the last of Gothic, which we call Perpendicular. But the intermediate stages are very interesting. The fine vault of St. George's, Windsor, shows shapes that are beginning to approximate to the fan vault; and there are two near-fan vaults at Oxford. In the Divinity School we get the conoids and the pendants, but the great transverse arches, which really uphold the stone roof, are prominently visible throughout. In the lovely vault of Oxford Cathedral quire, they pass, as at Westminster, behind the conoids; and the centre is filled with an intricate network of lierne ribs.

Take fan vaults proper. We have a typical instance in the nave of Sherborne. As at Oxford, the conoids do not go the whole width of the span, but give a space between filled with interlacing ribs. At King's College Chapel, Cambridge, the great transverse arches are clearly shown, but the trumpet shapes are so big and so close together that you never get the whole semicircle, and the effect is perhaps somewhat cut up and crowded. There are other examples, as at Bath; and it is great fun to look for chantries and tombs and see how they often have little fan vaults of their own. Undoubtedly it was an original stroke of the designers of the two Oxford vaults, and that of Westminster, to start the conoids some distance from the walls, so as to give something of an aisled effect, in which the pillars are replaced by pendants, and thus produce the illusion that the vault is floating in air.

The building of the Chapel was started by Henry VII in 1503; and in the front of the drawing is seen the bronze screen around his tomb. It was this tomb, not screen, that was the forerunner of the new Renaissance style; for Henry VIII entrusted the work to an Italian, Pietro Torrigiano (1516). If its details are examined, we shall find that we have here all the characteristic pilasters with caps, bases, and mouldings that are associated with Classic architecture. An illustration of this tomb is given in Vol. II. Henry VII's Chapel is a wonderful place—the vault represents the culmination of Gothic, and the tomb is typical of the re-birth of Classic design.

THE GROWTH OF THE LIBRARY

Fig. *169* shows the next development of the library. We have seen how in a Benedictine monastery the north walk of the cloisters was used for the purpose of study, small carrels being formed in the window openings on to the central garth, and the books being kept in wooden almeries, or cupboards, placed against the wall opposite the carrels. Books were also stored in an "armarium", which was a cupboard fitted up in a recess in the wall, generally between the chapter-house

169   A Chained Library

and the door into the church. The Cistercians sometimes cut off a space from the chapter-house, and stored books there; but they were taken to the cloister to be read. As the number of books increased, and the desire for knowledge became more general, these arrangements were found to be inconvenient; and the practice started of building separate rooms as libraries where the books could be both stored and studied. These were often added on the top of the cloisters, and were long narrow rooms, with windows spaced equally along the walls. Between the windows were set up, at right angles to the walls, desks rather like church lecterns, on which books were laid flat, and chained to a bar over, as shown in the sketch. This chaining shows the value of medieval books, and seems to indicate that the fifteenth-century student was not always very honest. A shelf, added to the underpart of the desks, was used for storage purposes; and between the desks were fixed strong benches.

Libraries were not large in those days. Mr. Willis Clark, in *The Care of Books*, speaking of College libraries, says that at King's Hall in 1397 only 87 volumes are enumerated; and even in the University Library not more than 122 volumes were recorded in 1424. These were mainly concerned with Theology, Philosophy, Medicine, Logic, Grammar, History, and Canon Law—all heavy reading.

The drawing serves to show how much alike all Gothic woodwork was; whether it was a church bench, library desk, or furniture for the house, the detail was much the same.

MILLERS AND MILLWRIGHTS

We now leave houses and buildings, to study the everyday things of country life. Our next illustration(*170*), is of a wind-mill—but it has been drawn from one still existing in Essex, and must not be taken as an exact representation of a fifteenth-century mill. Our drawing shows the traditional principle on which a mill works.

It is a Post Mill, like the one drawn for the fourteenth century(*131*). The old millwright first built the four piers shown as a foundation; on the tops of these were laid great oak beams; and then the large central post, formed from a single oak tree, was cut down over the beams and wedged up to them, and braced on four sides by the struts. All this part of the mill was enclosed by a round house, which, with the beams, struts, and central post, was a fixture; the rest of the mill, including the steps up to it, turned on the top of the post. The bearing on which the mill turned was formed between the large beam, shown just underneath the floor where the millstones are, and the post; and this is worth consideration, because the weight of the stones is arranged to come directly on to this large beam, and so prevents the mill becoming top-heavy, as would happen if the stones were one stage up.

Now, as to the way a windmill works. We have described in the fourteenth-century chapter how the sails are set duty rather like the screw of a steamer, that the wind may readily blow them round, and in so doing turn the main axle shown in the drawing. Next to the sails is a large gear-wheel, all framed up in wood, with cogs on its face made of pear wood; these engage with another cogged wheel, which turns the top stone, the lower one being a fixture. A smaller gear-wheel at the end of the axle engages another cogged wheel, which cannot be shown as it is behind the gear-wheel; and this, in its turn, is engaged with two other cogged wheels, each operating the upper stone of a pair of smaller mill-stones.

The next detail is the process of grinding the corn. From the back of the large gear-wheel on the main axle, a band is taken to shafting at the extreme top of the mill; and from this, by means of a fixed and loose pulley, a hoist is worked which brings up the sacks of corn to the topmost story, where the miller is shown emptying a sack into a bin. A funnel from the bottom of the bin leads to a shoot which conveys the corn to the stone. The slope of this shoot is adjustable, because different sorts of grain, peas, and beans will slide at different rates, and so will need different slopes to the shoot. Then they are further encouraged to slide down by the end of the shoot, which delivers into a hole in the centre of the top stone, having a little notch cut in it, which, as the spindle turns round, chatters against it, and so shakes the grain, or whatever it is, down to the stones to be ground. The flour comes out at the sides, and is conducted by other shoots either into sacks or into bins on the floor by the door where the miller is standing.

The body of the mill is framed up in timber, all built up on to the large beam under the stones, which turns on the top of the post, or is suspended from it. The post goes right up through the floor by the door where the man stands.

We now come to another very interesting subject of country life—Hunting. Most of our ancestors were great hunters, who encouraged every sport in which they could indulge in their favourite sport of stag-hunting. And it is probable that the huntsman of the Devon and Somerset hunting grounds to-day carries on the traditions that his forefathers produced. So it continued all through the Middle Ages. Men hunted for pleasure and for the satisfaction of being able to eat the game so provided, which came as a pleasant relief from their salted meat in the winter. We get an excellent idea of hunting at the end of the fourteenth and the beginning of the fifteenth centuries, from a book called The Master of Game, written by Edward, Duke of York, a grandson of Edward III, who was killed at Agincourt in 1415. He was Master of Game to Henry V, and so wrote as an authority. His book, though largely a translation from one published by Gaston de Foix, about 1390, called La Chasse, contains many vivid descriptions of English hunting.

1700 A Cut-away drawing of a Windmill

247

the post, or is suspended from it. The post goes right up through the floor by the door where the man stands.

Now we will suppose that the direction of the wind has changed in the night. The louvres on the sails have been opened, so that the wind blows through, and does not turn them round. When the miller starts work in the morning, the first thing to do is to get the mill into the wind, so one of his men goes down the steps, and pulls them up clear from the ground. The man at the bottom has his left hand on a long beam, which sticks out like a tail, and passes through the centre of the steps. This tail is fixed on to the floor beams at the bottom of the mill—not on to the centre post. The man at the bottom takes a ring on the end of a chain, and pops it over one of the small posts which are shown in a circle round the mill, and then winds up the tail towards the post, until he gets the mill into the wind. We shall see how, in a later century, this was done by a very clever automatic arrangement, which kept the mill always in its proper position. Windmills are wonderful things, rather like ships on land. The sails as they thrash round make a beautiful thrum-thrum in the air.

HUNTING

We now come to another interesting aspect of country life— Hunting. We have seen that the Normans were great hunters, who enclosed large tracts of land in which they could indulge in their favourite sport of stag-hunting; and it is probable that the huntsman of the Devon and Somerset staghounds to-day carries on the traditions that the Normans introduced. So it continued all through the Middle Ages; men hunted for pleasure and for the satisfaction of being able to eat the game so provided, which came as a pleasant relief from their salted meat in the winter. We get an excellent idea of hunting at the end of the fourteenth and the beginning of the fifteenth centuries, from a book called *The Master of Game*, written by Edward, Duke of York, a grandson of Edward III, who was killed at Agincourt in 1415. He was Master of Game to Henry VI, and so wrote as an authority. His book, though largely a translation from one published in France by Count Gaston de Foix, about 1390, called *La Chasse*, contains many vivid descriptions of English hunting.

HUNTING

Our Master of Game begins by describing the nature of the hare, in the second place that of the hart; the buck comes third; then follow the roe, wild boar, wolf, fox, badger, cat, marten; and the otter is eleventh. The wolf has gone; but the wild cat remains in the remote Highlands as a fierce and dangerous little beast. There follows an account of the hounds, raches or running hounds, greyhounds, alauntes, spaniels, mastiffs "that men call curs", and "small curs that fallen to be terriers"; and our Master goes on to talk of the care of hounds and their kennels. The greyhounds mentioned include what we should now call wolf- and deerhounds.

There is a beautiful description of the country, which shows that at the end of the fourteenth century the hunting-man took quite as much pleasure as he does now in the delights of being out in the open air, across a good horse, watching hounds at work.

Now shall I prove [our Master says] how hunters live in this world more joyfully than any other men, for when the hunter riseth in the morning, and he sees a sweet and fair morn and clear weather and bright, and he heareth the song of the small fowls, the which sing so sweetly with great melody and full of love, each in his own language in the best wise that he may, after that he may learn of his own kind. And when the sun is arisen, he shall see fresh dew upon the small twigs and grasses, and the sun by his virtue shall make them shine. And that is great joy and liking to the hunter's heart.

His picture of stag-hunting makes one remember happy days on Exmoor, with the meet at Cloutsham. There is the same discovery, or harbouring of the deer, by the huntsman with a hound, or lymer led on a line, as shown in our cut. A few hounds are uncoupled

171 A Lymer or Hound

249

to move on the deer as the hunters do nowadays; and the chase is taken up by delays of the pack called vame chasours, the middle, and the parfytours; and, at the finish, when the hounds are blooded, the huntsman is rewarded with good wine.

When our friend goes home the shall doff his clothes, and his shoes, and his hose, and he shall wash his thighs and his legs, and peradventure all his body. And in the meanwhile he shall order well his supper, with oilers of the neck of the hart and of other good meats, and good wine and ale"; and going to bed sleeps well and dreams of hunting, rested fastly without any evil thoughts of any sins, wherefore I say that hunters go into Paradise when they die, and live in this world more joyfully than any other men." Oh, good man, let us hope that he had a clean death at Agincourt, and found his dream come true!

Let us also hope that in the new England there will still be some room left for indulgence in the same joys, and that it won't be all uninteresting work and no play, for then we shall get such dull boys that they might even become vicious, and full of those "evil thoughts of sin" which our Master held to be so well driven out by hunting.

Our Master describes all the various kinds of hunting, always in the same delightful way, and with many quaint remarks, that help to give one an excellent idea of the life of the countryside. The meet is a much less business-like performance than nowadays; in fact, they appear to have started with a picnic.

The hare is described as a "good little beast, and there is much good sport and liking in the hunting of her more than any other beast", of the same size apparently. Stag-hunting, of course, came first, but the harriers of that day took the place of to-day's foxhounds. The hare was hunted much as it would be now by harriers; but the pack includes rathes, or scenting hounds, and greyhounds; and fig. 172 shows such a hunt in progress. They were also run down by greyhounds held leashed in couples, much as in modern coursing, on having been driven out of corn by greyhounds, were shot with the cross-bow; but these two methods appear to have been more French than English. Or they might be driven into nets by men holding a rope between them on which bells were suspended, or snared in enclosures with trapped entrances.

The fox is said to be a "common beast", and is regarded more

On the left ... was a small but thick shield of wood, covered with leather emblazoned with the short embroidered ... is or less as vermin, and was often smoked out, and taken in nets—a rather dreadful idea for fox-hunters. Badgers were dug out, as they are to-day in the West Country. We remember an amusing badger hunt in South Devon, which took place at night, with a very mixed pack and hunt. While footing it over that up-hill-and-down-dale country, with no more light than a bicycle-lamp gave, the hunt was widely distributed across the landscape; the deep lanes were full of flustered men who had fallen into them, and no one ever learned what happened to the badger. We do not know whether this style of hunting was a survival from the past; but, on that occasion, it did help to demonstrate the survival of the fittest.

THE TOURNAMENT

Hunting served as an excellent training for active service in the field, and the knights and squires engaged in tournaments for the same purpose. The joust, as we see in fig. 173, was a fight between two knights only, and the weapon used was the lance. These jousts came before, or after, a tourney. The arrangements for the "lists," where the fighting took place, were generally the same. A large oblong space was railed round, leaving an opening at either end for the entrance of the opposing parties, and here were the tents of the combatants. Seats were placed on one side for the judges and ladies, and on the other for ordinary folk. Through these latter seats was a third entrance.

Tournaments were very gay festivals; the company met together a day or two before the ceremony, and a great dance was held, with much feasting and mirth.

251

The knights fighting in the tourney wore armour somewhat different from that used in battle. It was heavier, and the large "heaume", surmounted by its beautiful crest and well-padded inside, was firmly strapped on to the breast- and back-plates. Several of these heaumes are still in existence in various collections, and nearly all weigh over 20 lb. As the rest of the tilting armour was of the same strength and thickness, a knight entering the lists must have been a magnificent but a very heavy and cumbersome figure indeed.

On the left breast and shoulder was fastened a small but thick shield of wood, covered with leather emblazoned with the wearer's arms. Over this armour, the knight often wore a short embroidered surcoat; and his horse, too, was clad in an emblazoned coat which nearly touched the ground. His head and neck were protected with chain armour and plates of steel.

Tourneys were fought with sword or mace. The sword used was round at the tip and blunted at the sides, and much resembled a plain bar of steel, and all blows were given with the flat, not the point. The object of the fight was not to pierce one's opponent but to unhorse him. So we can see the necessity of armour strong enough to withstand the force of heavy blows, and sufficiently padded to prevent injury to the wearer if he were thrown.

The mace was of wood, suspended by a cord fastened to a ring on the right of the breast-plate. The small wooden shield mentioned earlier, called the *manteau d'armes*, was worn for jousting, where the object was to strike one's opponent in the centre of this shield and unhorse him, or else to shiver his lance. These shields were made concave, that the blow might glance off and outwards. The combatants used lances with blunted ends, with three small projections but no points.

A knight often rode in a joust bearing his lady's sleeve fastened to his right arm. These were made of fur, or long embroidered pieces of stuff which ladies wore fastened over the tight under-sleeve. You can see pictures of them in almost any fourteenth- or fifteenth-century illustration.

If the combatants were not unhorsed at the first encounter, they could return to the end of the lists and charge twice more, and their squires waited there, ready, after every charge, to

173   A Joust between Knights in the time of Henry VI

change their lances or any piece of armour that might have been damaged.

On the open ground at one end of the lists the tents of the challengers were erected, and at the other end were those of the knights who took up the challenge. The ceremony was as follows: the challengers hung their shields outside their tents, and any knight wishing to accept the challenge rode up and touched a shield with his lance, thus showing his willingness to fight with the owner.

In the illustration the herald is seen standing in the lists, holding, instead of two shields, "two saddles of choyes". These saddles belong to the knights who are fighting.

At the end of the jousts, the winner was awarded a prize by one of the ladies, who had been named the Queen of Beauty for the occasion.

A PUPPET SHOW AND RELIGIOUS DRAMA

The next illustration (174) is of a puppet show, such as might have been found at a tourney, to amuse the people between the various encounters of the knights.

Very little is known of early puppet shows, but that there were such things is proved by illustrations in old manuscripts. In Cervantes's tale of *Don Quixote*, written at the end of the sixteenth century, there is an account of a puppet show, in which was enacted the tale of a Spanish knight who rescued his lady from the Moors. Many puppets would appear to have been manipulated in these scenes; and the book speaks of the showman behind, working the little figures, while a boy stood in front pointing with a wand to each puppet as he told the tale. Performing animals, especially apes, were exhibited by the puppet showmen, who travelled from place to place, giving an exhibition of their skill in every neighbourhood they came to.

It must always be remembered that, since very few people could read in the Middle Ages, shows and signs were an important method of communication. The inns had a bush hanging outside, from which we get the saying that "Good wine needs no bush", and other traders used signs, which came to be generally recognised as an advertisement of what they had to sell. The priests made use of a similar method,

and taught their
congregation Bible
history by acting be-
fore them stories
from its pages, too,
in the same way,
showed incidents in
the life of one of the
saints. These were
called Mystery or
Miracle Plays. They
were of very early
origin, for William
Fitzstephen (p. 40),
in his life of Thomas
à Becket (1182),
writes of represen-
tations of miracles
worked by holy
confessors or the
sufferings wherein
was demonstrated
the endurance of
martyrs. Later on,
the plays became
very elaborate, and
were formed into a
collection, or Cycle, beginning with the Creation and ending
with the Last Judgment, like the cycle of carved bosses on the
nave vault of Norwich Cathedral (described on page 171). The
plays, Norwich bosses, and much of the sculpture in the
cathedrals served this same purpose of educating people who
could not read. The Easter Sepulchre, which we find in
churches, was designed for a representation of the Entombment
of our Lord. The plays were given in the church porch, or
churchyard, and sometimes on a car which could be moved
about.

Morality plays date from the fifteenth century, and deal with
such themes as the fight of Vice against Virtue for the possession
of the human soul. This was the drama of the Middle Ages,

which after the Renaissance was to be developed by the genius of Shakespeare into the modern play.

DECORATION

As a typical fifteenth-century manuscript(*167*) we have chosen a page that is entirely decorative; it is the opening page of Psalm 110, from a Psalter of about 1420: "The Lord said unto my lord." The graceful ornament is very like that of the *St. Omer Psalter* in the British Museum (Add. MS. 39800); if not by the same hand, it belongs to the same school. The pages from *Admiral Coetivy's Hours* have delicate running ornament; but the flowers, such as columbines and strawberries, are becoming naturalistic and are not so intimately woven into the background. This heralds the decadent later style, when pinks, strawberries, violets, and other flowers, with butterflies and snails, were painted realistically all round the border without any attempt at a formal design. Still later manuscripts show Renaissance forms; and then came the printing press and the death of the illuminator's art.

We can only touch very briefly on the illuminations we have arranged as illustrations to our four chapters. Notice how the Bayeux Tapestry(*18, 19*) resembles manuscript work of the time(*70*) when reduced. The medical drawings(*30–3*) show the effective outline work, slightly shaded, of the end of the twelfth or early thirteenth century; and we have already referred to the similar, but rather later, MS. at Trinity College, Cambridge (p. 48). The marvellous thirteenth-century *Majekowski MS.* is probably the greatest masterpiece of its time; and the Roxburgh club facsimile should be studied. Its long history of Eastern wanderings makes a romantic and enthralling tale; £200 was recently paid for a single stray leaf. Figs. *126–9* from the Bodleian library shows, enmeshed in typical ornament, some of those delightful little marginal drawings that picture for us so graphically life and work in the Middle Ages. Nine varied, but representative, miniature paintings of the fifteenth century are seen on figs. *141–2, 150, 151–2, 164–6, 167.*

The tailpiece shows a design used in the West of England in this century on church screens; and the significance of the vine in such a situation does not need explaining. The main lines of the pattern are wavy, like the tailpiece to the twelfth-century chapter; but it is far more elaborate and more natural in its treatment. Yet it is a design, and not just a drawing of a vine, grapes, and birds. The various parts are spaced so as to form what is called the "repeat", which means the unit that by repetition forms the whole pattern. It is the arrangement of these repeats, and the way in which they fill up the space to be decorated, that spell the success, or failure, of the design; the repeat may be interesting in itself and yet not good when it occurs again and again. Another interesting point is that sometimes the spaces left between the design are as important, from the decorative point of view, as the design itself.

This is our last pattern of the Gothic period; and in Vol. II we shall be beginning a new Renaissance series from which it will be clear that both Gothic and Renaissance designers went back to the same source of inspiration. Both borrowed from the ancient world. After the fall of the Roman Empire in the West, various nations adopted her architecture, and developed the ruder style we now call "Romanesque", from which our own "Norman" came. In 1453, when the Turks captured Constantinople, where the Roman classical tradition had been carried on, the scholars whom they drove out took this same classical tradition to Italy, and there started the Renaissance, or rebirth of the old Greek and Roman forms, in Art and Literature. This new movement travelled across France, and found its way to England in the early days of Henry VIII's reign. Our task in Vol. II is to show how it influenced everyday things from Tudor days down to the end of the eighteenth century.

175   "Perpendicular" Pattern

INDEX

The numerals in **heavy type** refer to the *figure numbers* of the illustrations

INDEX

INDEX